D0481602

# FIVE WOMEN I LOVE

# FIVE WOMEN
# I LOVE

*Bob Hope's Vietnam Story*

*By* BOB HOPE

DOUBLEDAY & COMPANY, INC.
GARDEN CITY, NEW YORK
1966

DEDICATED

WITH RESPECT AND AFFECTION

TO

THE REAL AUTHORS OF THIS BOOK:

THE GALLANT MEN AND WOMEN OF

OUR ARMED FORCES

Library of Congress Catalog Card Number 66–28863
Copyright © 1966 by Bob Hope
All Rights Reserved
Printed in the United States of America
First Edition

# PREFACE

For the past year, D & D, the publishers, have been dunning me to write this book about Vietnam. Since then we made another visit, and I suppose soon after this book is out we'll get a third chance in the Rice Belt.

I didn't really want to write a book . . . but the Government heard there was money in it. And I certainly don't need any extra work, because now I do personal appearances, television, radio, movies, albums, and in the fringe areas you can get me on rotisseries. It was quite a job, doing this book. I'd write anywhere—on tablecloths—napkins—that's why Chapter Twelve is a little skinny. It didn't come back from the laundry. My wife read the manuscript and enjoyed it. She said I write like O'Hara. How about that? I didn't know Maureen could write.

I have evolved as the recognized world authority on one contemporary subject—me. And it's occurred to me that if I'm gonna have anything at all that I enjoy reading, I'd better get busy and write it.

Moreover, I must be a sucker for a uniform. I have no other way of explaining how I became Mary Poppins to the military.

Somewhere inside me there's a cherished and indestructible memory of my first soldier audience. I looked at them, they laughed at me, and it was love at first sight. For some strange reason which escapes me, where the boys are is not always the most convenient location. Lately we've had a group spread across Vietnam and Southeast Asia, and getting to 'em makes an Apollo mission look like a wedge shot.

On our last junket we covered twenty-three thousand miles in thirteen days and even Chrysler won't guarantee your parts for that kind of action. But while getting there may not be half the fun, it's when you arrive that things really start popping. Like the hotel, the airport—in fact, there's hardly any place you may not get a big bang out of. But these joys are as nothing compared with that tidal wave of affection that wells up out of an audience of our fighting men. And fighting men they are. Although lately some of them don't even appear to be grown up enough for Granny Goose. In spite of that they're doing a magnificent job under unbelievably difficult conditions. Not knowing where the enemy is or who's firing at you can be unnerving. Not knowing where your friends or the people back home stand can be shattering. That it hasn't been is a tribute to the brave men I was proud to meet.

It is to these courageous kids that this book is dedicated.

When I think of some of the far-out places we found them, in the rain, mud, and stifling heat, I have nothing but respect and compassion.

And when I realize that another group tolerated the same hardships for the purpose of bringing them a little cheer, I have a confession to make—I'm in love with five women.

Now that the cats are out of the bag, I might as well go whole hog and tip my mitt. Not only am I in love with five women, but I add five to the group every year. And it's been going on for some time. Let me pull up a couch and tell you about it.

# ACKNOWLEDGMENTS

I would like to express my sincere appreciation to the Department of Defense, especially to Major General Joseph E. Lambert of the Professional Entertainment Branch and his staff, backed up by individual Special Service officers of the Army, Air Force, Navy, and Marines all along the way.

Another word of thanks is due the U.S.O., whose dedicated support has been so helpful to our tours, and especially for the magnificent job they have done in continuing to provide entertainment for our troops overseas.

I am grateful to NBC for permission to use the photographs by Frank Carroll and Gary Null; also to United Press International Telephoto; and to Charles Moore, Curtis Publishing Company.

*It's not often I look down on the President.* (*UPI Telephoto*)

# CHAPTER ONE

The President was staring at me. The next thing I knew I had my foot in my mouth on three networks. It was in March of 1965, Wednesday, the thirty-first to be exact, a date that comes easily to my mind because it happens to be engraved on my eyeballs. We were in the International Ballroom at the Washington Hilton for the U.S.O. Silver Anniversary Dinner and some twelve hundred people, a really distinguished crowd, were there. As I looked around at all those important, famous, and highly trusted Government executives, I couldn't help wondering which one's gonna leak all the details to Drew Pearson.

John Daly was doing a great job as emcee and about a half hour earlier he had looked down at me and said, "I'm in trouble." I know John is usually very cool and collected and has any kind of situation well in hand. If John was in trouble, something was happening.

"I just got a message that the President is leaving the White House at ten o'clock," John continued. "He will be here at ten-ten, and must go on immediately. After all, we don't leave the President standing in the wings, do we?"

I thought he was putting me on, because I had spoken to the White House earlier about going over to visit with the Man the following day, and they said the President thought he might go to the U.S.O. dinner, but it was very unlikely that his schedule would permit it. I had put the whole thing out of my mind and was barely conscious of John Daly rearranging the whole program. Then suddenly John said, "Ladies and gentlemen, the President of the United States," and the whole room jumped to its feet, and there he was walking on and taking over the show, and to my amazement, what he had to say was very intimately concerned with me. He said:

"Mr. Chairman, Mr. Hope, ladies and gentlemen, I have come here today to honor a man with two very unusual traits. He is an actor who is not, so far as I know now at least, running for public office."

He got a big laugh and applause. I had mixed emotions. I was delighted that he had singled me out but bugged that he had killed two jokes in my imminent monologue. He continued:

"And he is a frequent visitor to Vietnam, who has never been asked to testify before the Senate Foreign Relations Committee. At least, not yet. I understand he was planning to testify until he discovered there was live coverage on only one network. And it wasn't the friendly network. It isn't that he wanted the additional exposure, it was just that he refused to go up against 'I Love Lucy''s rating without some help. It may come as a surprise to some people with short memories that Bob Hope is more than a comedian. He is also a best-selling author. The book about his travels to entertain our troops during the Second World War led the best-seller list back there in 1944. It was called *I Never Left Home*. Since then he has spent so much time with our troops overseas that there are those who now say he oughta write a sequel. He could call this one, *I Never Came Back*.

"Bob, we are very glad that you came back long enough to be with us tonight. The courageous and dedicated young men who laugh with you in Vietnam today have fathers who laughed with you from Europe to the South Pacific in World War II. And when the U.S.O. was founded twenty-five years ago, Hope was there. And he is here tonight.

And we all know that wherever American men fight for freedom, there will always be Hope. And, Bob, two generations of Americans raise their glasses and say to you, 'Thanks for the Memories.'

"This plaque is to Bob Hope and says, 'Thanks for the Memory from a grateful nation.'"

If I seem immodest in recounting these details, let me add that the President said other things so flattering, it's embarrassing for me to put them down in print. But where are you other journalists when I need you??

Anyhow, it was my turn to get up and reply, and if John Daly thought *he* was in trouble, how about me?

A lot of my material was written about the Administration and wasn't exactly a testimonial. Let's face it, I need two or three days of careful rehearsal before I can ad lib a new monologue. I was still trying desperately to think of an opening line as he handed me the award. I finally said, "Thank you very much, Mr. President." Not too clever, but I was on safe ground so far. My next line was: "Pretty crazy drop-in, isn't he?" And when they roared, a little of my confidence came back. I decided to forge on. I said, "It's nice to be here in Washington—or as the Republicans call it, 'Camp Runamuck.' . . . But it's nice to be back here in Birdland." . . . That's when he stared at me. I stared back, and I felt the chicken in me rising. I leaned over and said to him, "I have to do it, sir—it's on the paper." When the audience heard that limp little disclaimer, they roared. I was sure that any minute the Immigration Department would be paying me a visit, and I looked over cautiously at the Prez to see how he was taking it. He loved it. Not only that, but each time I'd do a joke about him, he would time his stare at me. . . . It was as though he was timing his reaction to help me get the laugh. . . . Not that I needed it. But it was kind of a "Saver." He knew exactly what I was doing, playing against him . . . and he would slowly look up at me and hold it until the laugh belted in.

For a brief moment I had an idea of astonishing possibilities . . . but then I dismissed it. . . . I don't really think he'd make a *Road* picture with me.

I was sailing along pretty good and when I said, "I wouldn't want to miss Washington this time of the year, because it's wonderful with the cherry blossoms and Senator Morse's mustache all in bloom." . . .

That's a pretty fair joke, but what made it hilarious was right then LBJ put his other hand up to his head. I knew right then that next to President Johnson, Millard Fillmore was just a straight man. I had a few other targets and the Prez's reactions kept building. Like when I made reference to Toastmaster John Daly and the other distinguished guests:

"Before I forget, I want to acknowledge John Daly, who is under contract to the U.S.O. to be Toastmaster forever, I think. And he's always so great . . . such a gentleman, and polite and charming. How he ever made good in television I'll never know.

"No, he really surprised me with what a great job he did here tonight. After all, he's new at standing up, and I think it's just wonderful.

"I had a wonderful day. I went out with Stu Symington and Admiral Raborn and Dan Kimball, and we played at Burning Tree today. And I was on every tee in regulation, and we had a wonderful day.

"And I wanna tell you that Dan Kimball plays the greatest golf, but he's a little wild. He got up to the first hole, hit one in the woods, then on the ninth hole he hit one into the lake, and on the next hole he hit a new ball into the woods again, and I said, 'Dan, why don't you use an old ball?' and he said, 'I never had one.'

"And it's nice to see Father Bunn of Georgetown U. here. As John told you, I did get a degree at Georgetown when my son graduated, and I want to thank him again for that.

In fact, I've had five honorary degrees. I've been a doctor so many times, I'm starting to resent Medicare."

Right about there I looked over at the Prez to see if I had touched a nerve, but he was still digging it. I was tempted to say, "The President is a wonderful sport. I've kidded him a lot on my jokes but he's never said one word about it. And my passport is still good everywhere in the world . . . except for Texas." But I didn't want to press my luck. I went on with the routine:

"This is a very sentimental occasion for me. The U.S.O. and I have been going steady for twenty-five years. It's the nicest travel agency I've ever had. They handle more actors than the Republican Party. . . .

"And I'm proud to receive this award from the President. Of course, I didn't expect anything so elaborate. I thought they'd just have my first box lunch bronzed.

"It's a thrilling, thrilling dinner for me, and I'd come back just to shake hands with all the wonderful people here tonight. So many of the people that I've worked with.

"I've never seen so much brass. I really haven't. Took me two hours just to salute my way out of the washroom just now.

"And I'm thrilled to see Joan Crawford here. And, after all, as you know, Anita Bryant was with us, and you know she's the Coca-Cola girl. In fact, we had to burp her every three days. And, of course, Joan is here picking up a few empties for Pepsi-Cola. And I'm here for Alka-Seltzer, so we're all right."

After my remark about Joan Crawford I glanced over at her and I was thrilled. This radiantly beautiful woman seemed to have discovered the secret of staying young, and, as usual, she looked every inch the star. Aside from the Balmain she was wearing that must have cost quite a few bottle caps, she was adorned with an acre of diamonds. With all that ice flashing on her, she looked like a living chandelier. It was lucky she wasn't sitting next to LBJ

13

*Worst rash I ever had. (NBC Photo by Frank Carroll)*

. . . you know how he is about lights. But back to my pearls. I continued:

"I know the U.S.O. has done a lot for me. How else would I be able to go on trips with gals like Lana Turner, Jayne Mansfield, Janis Paige, Carroll Baker, and Anita Bryant, and have my wife pack my lunch?

"And I appreciate the nice things that General Rosie O'Donnell said about me. He's one of the toughest men our Air Force ever had. Of course, with a name like 'Rosie,' he had to be.

"But he really is tough. He gets fan mail from John Wayne.

"In 1950 I stayed at the General's pad at Ukoto when he was head of the bombers over there, and it's very nice if you don't mind sleeping at attention. I had a wonderful time. And he loaned me a pair of his pajamas. It's murder at night when you roll over on those cold medals, I wanna tell you that.

"But he's done a great job for the U.S.O. And he's very thorough. Before he sends them overseas, he spends hours auditioning the belly dancers.

"Thanks to his efforts, Goose Bay is warmer than Miami Beach.

"No, and Rosie has always been very helpful to us in helping us get the planes and things when we want to go on these trips. In fact, he wanted to make sure we had the modern equipment. The last one, I think, belonged to a four-star General. Pershing.

"This plane was so old, Richard Arlen was flying it.

"I mean, I don't mind an open cockpit, but when you have to go out on the wing to the restroom, that's too much.

"Outside of this wonderful occasion, there's another purpose in me coming to Washington. And I want to thank the guy who made all those phone calls and got my Vietnam show a top rating.

"Is he around? This fellow claimed that he raised the rating of my Christmas show three points because he likes me. Never mind the Christmas show. If he wants to help me, why doesn't he work on my golf score?

"The way things are going, I expect to read that World War II was rigged.

"That's not funny, these are news events.

"No, the news came as a shock to me. We flew fifty thousand miles and here a guy standing in a phone booth did it all.

"If he's got that much influence, I wish he'd make one more phone call for me . . . to the Academy Awards Committee.

"Incidentally, he's not rigging ratings any more. He now has a steady job. He's working for the Republicans.

"And it's nice to see my dear friend, Senator Stu Symington here. The last time I saw him was in Danang. Okay, as the guys over there call it, 'Dodge City.'

"Stu Symington met us in Vietnam with a telegram from President Johnson. That's what happens when you elect a Texan President. Anybody else would have called Western Union.

"We had a film clip of the Senator on our television show, and he was a big hit. He looks a lot like that fellow in the Granny Goose commercial.

"No, Stu is one of the handsomest men in this country. Fortunately, he doesn't tell jokes or the resemblance would be too much to bear.

"He's not only a great statesman, but a helluva politician. He's the only Missourian I know with a Texas drawl.

"And I'll never forget how Stu got me to go to Alaska. He told me how much the fellows up there liked me, and how funny they thought I was, and how they were all dying to see my act. And one snow job led to another, and there I was trying to find my toes.

"And I want to congratulate Stu. I understand his son,

16

Jim, has just been appointed Chief of Protocol. It just proves that blood is thicker than Civil Service.

"I wish him a lot of luck. I really do, because it's a very sensitive job. He has to tell the President what names are all right to call DeGaulle.

"And he arranged that wonderful welcome for Mrs. Gandhi. It wasn't easy to get Senator Fulbright to lie on a bed of nails.

"I owe a lot to the U.S.O. Thanks to them I've been to such exciting spots as Guadalcanal, Korea, Santo Domingo, and Saigon. You've made me a hero and my insurance man a millionaire.

"But there's so many exotic places I never would have gotten to without the U.S.O. . . . also diseases.

"It's a wonderful organization. They've done more for the men of our country than anyone since Zsa Zsa Gabor.

"Twenty-five years. Just think, Cassius Clay was just born. A six-pound mouth.

"Wasn't that a shame about Cassius? He opened his mouth and got caught in the draft?

"The whole thing gives me a warm feeling.

"I just want to say the U.S.O. has a sneaky way of letting me know when I'm going on a tour. Once a year they send over a guy who says, 'Bend over, Mr. Hope . . . this won't hurt a bit.'

"Last time he didn't wait until I got my pants off. I've got the only wallet in town that's immune to malaria.

"I can't give enough praise to our den mother, whom you heard up here, Anita Bryant. She actually is the youngest den mother in history. But she's a great gal.

"We had five beautiful gals like that, and I hope you saw them on the show. The general who said, 'War is hell' should have made the trip with us, that's all.

"Actually, the girls were never in danger at any time. Those MPs never took their eyes off me for a minute.

"Of course, some people don't think the U.S.O. should

*"Why do they whistle when I come out, Mr. Hope?"* (NBC Photo by Gary Null)

send pretty girls overseas, because they get the fellows too excited. I think that's ridiculous. I think the fellows should see what they're fighting for.

"I say this because a preacher named Bob Harrington from Bourbon Street in New Orleans recently came back from Vietnam and said we shouldn't send any more sexy girls over there. I just found out the name of his congregation. It's called 'Party Poopers.'

"I don't know why he's complaining. I've been down to Bourbon Street, and it's not exactly a boulevard of Phyllis Dillers.

"The last guy Phyllis stirred up was Batman. He took one look and flew away.

"But I'm glad we have the kind of guys over there who do get excited when they see a pretty girl. It's comforting to know that when the Cong wave a white flag our boys don't wave back. Thank God the only fliers we've got over there are in planes.

"We played to some of the toughest troops in the world, and the guys have never been anything but courteous. Of course, I know what they were thinking, but if you could be arrested for that, this war would be taking place in Leavenworth.

"There's a fellow sitting here that I would like to have take a bow, because Abe Lastfogel will agree with me, and George Chandler, that this fellow does an all-around great job. I think he's been to Korea and Japan four times. . . . He's been to Vietnam a couple of times, but outside of that he's a very helpful fellow in our cause. He's a wonderful guy, and a great disc jockey, and I'd like to have him take a bow . . . Mr. Johnny Grant. That's the 'Jackie Gleason of Tokyo,' we call him, and he's a wonderful fellow.

"I can't say enough for the boys over there. I know you know all about it, it's in all the papers. It's a tough war. Perry Mason was over there and even he couldn't solve it.

"And I want to tell you that Martha Raye did a marvel-

*Like they say, it's a shooting war. (NBC Photo by Gary Null)*

ous job. She really had a ball. She couldn't do enough for the boys.

"I think Vietnam actually left me a little nervous, because this morning my Wheaties popped and I surrendered to the maid.

"But there's one fellow out there that we should have heard from, and I was surprised that John didn't introduce him to sing a song, because there's nobody with his particular style, because it all started back in 1941 at March Field. This fellow was with me when we did our first camp show, and he's been with me ever since, and he's a great companion and a great American. Mr. Jerry Colonna. Where's Jerry? There he is!

"I just want to tell you that this award . . . I don't need this award, really I don't, I've had my kicks, I've been paid off so many, many hundreds of times in emotional thrills, with the contact with these most important guys in our country. And just getting this is an anticlimax, you know? The hard thing to do would be keeping me from making these trips. Because these servicemen audiences and those big laughs are like opium to me. And every December I call the Pentagon and say, 'Book me somewhere, quick. I need a fix!'

"But I accept this award in the spirit in which it was given. I shall ignore entirely the fact it was given to me for leaving the country.

"That's the story of my career. The first time in twenty years that I didn't make a picture I got an Oscar for being a humanitarian.

"Last month the B'nai B'rith gave me an award for being a Christian.

"I can hardly wait to break a leg . . . it might mean a Nobel prize.

"I just want to acknowledge all the people on the show . . . Les Brown, and, of course, for me this is a great, great thrill being here, and, of course, having our President here to make this award just makes the year for me, and I know the sacrifice that he made, you know, because just leaving the store alone like that, with no one to watch Senator Morse . . . I think it's a marvelous thing. And I know he gave up a lot to be here tonight . . . a George Hamilton movie . . ."

As soon as I was finished, the President got up, which triggered everybody else in the room. I thanked him and he said, "I've really enjoyed it, and please come over and visit me tomorrow at the White House around noon, and bring anybody you want with you." For a brief instant I thought about selling tickets but I discarded that. I was lucky enough my speech hadn't gotten me arrested.

The next day Jerry Colonna, Johnny Grant, my PR man Bill Faith, and my son Tony joined me at the President's pad, and he gave us the full dollar-and-a-quarter tour. He took us out to the golf green where Ike used to practice and said:

"You've probably practiced here with Ike many times."

I said, "No, I've never practiced with Ike, but I've played with him and I must say the General plays like a real military man. Every time he gets on the green, he strokes the ball toward the hole and he yells, 'Fall in!'"

And the President laughed. I've worked for the last five Presidents and they all seemed to enjoy ad libbing—and getting a few laughs and hearing a few jokes. Like the time I did the joke about Mrs. Roosevelt at the White House Correspondents Dinner back in 1944, when I said:

"I understand that Mr. Roosevelt has been conferring with Winston Churchill on war strategy—war strategy meaning when and where will we attack the enemy and how will we keep Eleanor out of the cross fire."

President Roosevelt loved that joke and after the dinner, we met and talked and he said:

"That was a very funny joke and I'm going to tell it to Eleanor the next time I *write* to her."

And when Harry Truman heard me say that "he runs the country with an iron hand and plays the piano the same way," he countered with:

"I've heard you sing, and it would take an iron hand to get you on key."

Volumes have been written on the humor of John F. Kennedy. My favorite anecdote is the line he did at the Alfalfa Club Dinner in Washington, just after he was sworn in. He got up and stole the dinner with this one line:

"A lot of people are complaining about me appointing my brother as Attorney General, but I want to ask you one question: What's wrong with him getting a little legal practice before he goes into business for himself?"

And LBJ is pretty hip, too. As we walked back into the White House, I noticed there were still holes in the floor from the spikes on Ike's golf shoes. I speculated to the President that perhaps they hadn't been filled in out of reverence. Was this the beginning of a shrine? He said:

"No. We just don't want to do it on our budget."

We laughed. After all, it was *his* room.

I guess I never will get used to the security that surrounds the President. The White House is the only place where you can be followed into a washroom and not start a rumor. But it was immediately obvious that all the talk about economizing is true. I wanted to wash my hands, but I didn't have a coin for the slot.

But like a true Texan, LBJ's got stereo everywhere, and it can be embarrassing. How'd you like to be washing your hands when the speaker blasts out "The Eyes of Texas Are Upon You"?? I got so shook up I put back three towels.

I enjoyed the entire tour, however, and I must say the White House is in great shape—except for the holes under the President's desk. You know how some executives doodle? LBJ drills for oil.

Before we left, Johnny Grant wanted the President to sign a telegram that he had sent him in Vietnam. The President reached for one of his monogrammed ballpoints and tried to sign it, but it was dry. He tried with another one and that was also dry. I had the feeling that Prez was hoping Lady Bird would run out of wedding invitations before he ran out of pens. He finally got the telegram signed, and we posed for some pictures with him. We took so many, I now have more pictures of Lyndon than I do of my wife Dolores.

An interesting thing happens when you're posing for a picture with the President. You try to play it very casual, like it's something you do all the time, but underneath you're thinking:

"It'll be nice to have this picture when the Internal Revenue man comes around. . . . I could just sort of casually drop it on my W-2 Form. . . . Or . . . if I stand on the right side, will I get top billing when the newspaper caption says, 'Reading from left to right' . . . ? Or . . . this is really the President's lighting; I wonder if I can retouch just me."

After the picture-taking, he very graciously gave us some gifts, including an autographed copy of his book *My Hope for America,* and I was extremely flattered that I showed up in the title.

I'll always remember this visit to the White House because it put the icing on one of the high spots of my life. Although giving me an award for entertaining servicemen is like giving Richard Burton a medal for staying home, this occasion gave me an opportunity to relive some unforgettable experiences, and none have been more exciting than the 1965 Christmas trip.

Along about September each year, that tingle in the air is not the first sign of autumn in the San Fernando Valley. It's the annual stirring among my staff concerning where the Defense Department is sending us this year. Each summer the Joint Chiefs of Staff gather with the U.S.O. and commiserate, "He got back okay last Christmas . . . okay, let's try harder." Then they drop little pieces of paper listing all the world's trouble spots into a hat, and humming choruses from *Macbeth* they stir gently. That's how they managed to come up the last two years with Vietnam.

Saigon in '64 wasn't too bad, but in '65 it was for keeps. Victor Charley, a local resident who is something of a spoilsport, had fallen into the habit of booby-trapping everything from baubles and bangles to bagels. You think Hilton makes hotels go up fast—you should see what this group does. Naturally, I was delighted to be held over, if for no other reason than that this was an excellent opportunity to recharge my jungle rot. Fortunately, the destination is top secret because I am a prime target for the Viet Cong. Why should they be different?

So the news of our leaving only turns up in two or three gossip columns, which no self-respecting Communist would be caught dead reading. But the minute the decision is made, monumental preparations have to be begun.

We usually leave about the middle of December, and a month before that we send out our two advance men, Johnny Pawlek and Silvio Caranchini. Sil is my top assistant on the television shows and Johnny is my sound engineer, and they make the whole trip before we get there to insure that all provisions necessary for seeing and hearing our performance are made. Occasionally, after Pawlek has painstakingly planted speakers in such a way as to make a hangar acoustically acceptable, some General will inspect the premises and say, "Who left all this stuff laying around?" And then everything gets moved so that the audience has to be lip-readers. Sil collects poop material in each of the bases and sends it on to the writers. It usually arrives after the show. Which works out fine because then we have it in plenty of time for next year. Only next year they send us to all new bases.

We're usually strapped for time right before we leave on our annual Christmas tour, and rehearsals somehow always look like the out-of-town run-through of *Marat-Sade*. Only their madhouse is much better organized. Ours goes something like this:

Butch Stone hands out all of Joey Heatherton's music to the members of the band. The first violinist is about to set Les's arm operating for the downbeat when somebody notices that Joey Heatherton hasn't arrived yet. Kaye Stevens announces that she's ready to rehearse her numbers. Joey's music is collected. Jerry Null is taking some pre-departure shots. Onnie Morrow hands out shot record

*The Happy Rolling Rockheads. Clearance from the Board of Health just came through. (NBC Photo by Gary Null)*

cards with lists of what shots will be required for this trip. Les gives the downbeat. Kaye Stevens launches into her first number. Unfortunately the band is playing the shot record cards. One of the medicos, not expecting the downbeat, misses Les's arm and gives his shot to the first violinist. During this, Jack Jones, Jerry Colonna, and I are rehearsing a parody on "England Swings" in which we portray a singing group called "The Happy Rolling Rockheads." Gig Henry works feverishly on the lyrics while he complains that I don't sound at all like Roger Miller. Our makeup man, Mike Moschella, is auditioning a group of wigs which we rotate among us. The one that catches my fancy brings a scream of protest as I try to remove it from Colonna's head. How did I know he wasn't wearing one?

Colonel "Red" Beasley passes out security forms to all the cast. Onnie passes out blood type cards. Jan King passes out tangerines from my ranch in Palm Springs. The Nicholas Brothers finish their dance and just pass out. Johnny Rapp, modeling one of Carroll Baker's gowns, nearly gets arrested. Two groups of photographers are busy. The Air Force photographers appear to be taking pictures of the Air Force photographers. Probably from *Pravda*. Joey Heatherton arrives and they try to get some stills of her. Getting stills of Joey is impossible. She moves faster than the stock market and in more directions.

Anita Bryant arrives with Coca-Cola for everybody. Diana Lynn Batts poses for some cheesecake, and the medics, blinded by the flashes, give cholera shots to some, Coca-Cola shots to others. Anita hits a high note with the assistance of our costume designer, Kate Drain Lawson, who is pinning up her gown at the time.

Onnie Morrow, whose name seems to crop up often enough in these proceedings, has quite a bit to do with coordinating this overseas operation. This is the girl who, nine years ago, in one week got married, worked on the release of my movie *Alias Jesse James*, worked on the current television show, and took off on the overseas show. Her husband John saw pictures of the trip in March and was delighted to learn how he'd spent his honeymoon.

The busiest guy through the rehearsals is Barney McNulty, sometimes known as the King of the Idiot Card men. It's no secret by now, I'm sure, that actors can't memorize the mass of material television spews into your living room.

In the beginning Teleprompter was used extensively. This was a roller towel device hinged above the camera lens with the script printed on it, and it exposed a line or two as it rotated. The motion, I believe, conveyed a sense of urgency which often led to panic, for me, anyway, as I saw my jokes disappearing around the bend before I had a chance to tell them properly. Of course, the thing was motor-driven and could be slowed up by an operator, but I kind of hated the idea of my joke-timing being dictated by some kid with a rheostat in his hand, especially since it might be Bing's kid.

Then I discovered Barney, who prints the material in three-inch letters on cardboard, holds it nice and still, and laughs at all the jokes, and we eloped to Las Vegas. Barney has been with me ever since and the logistics of his operation in connection with one of our Christmas shows is staggering.

One year, Al Borden, our prop man (he's worth a whole book and I'll get to him in a minute), told Barney to load the cards in the wrong truck. That was the year we went to Korea and our idiot cards went to the Rose Bowl game. Sometimes the cards get there and Barney doesn't. That happened in Naples when I walked out to do my monologue and discovered that McNulty had taken the sight-seeing tour to Vesuvius. Occasionally the cards and Barney are both there and it still does you no good because he's taking pictures. Then I have to ad lib until he's got enough film for whatever movie it is he's shooting.

Jimmy Durante used to say, "I'm surrounded by assassins." It probably applies to me more than him. Take the chap referred to above, Al Borden. If you're old enough, you may remember a bit of doggerel that goes,

> *"Lizzie Borden took an ax*
> *And gave her mother forty whacks.*
> *Then to make sure the job was done*
> *She gave her father forty-one."*

I don't know if a blood relationship exists, there's certainly a spiritual one.

*This is what I call a foursome. Glamor—even in the snow.* (*NBC Photo by Frank Carroll*)

On at least two occasions "The Brain Surgeon," as we lovingly call him, almost had me. Once in Burbank he dropped a champagne bucket from the fly gallery that nicked my ear before carving a new trapdoor in the stage. And in Alaska, for a bit in which Ginger Rogers was to crease my skull with a breakaway bottle, Al supplied so-called breakaway bottles that are still being studied by our military for bullet-proofing material. My skull gave a little, but the bottles are still intact.

Borden's reaction to little mishaps like this has become a catchphrase on our show. With troubled eyes that mask

29

a secret smile, he says, "I don't understand it—it worked okay in the shop." Unfortunately, we don't do our show in the shop.

Some year, I guess, we'll put on a special called "The Best of Al Borden," and then we can use all the footage of his appearances on camera when a prop failed. He even turned up once in a dream that one of my writers, Bill Larkin, had. Bill says he dreamed he had a fight with Borden and when Al went to hit him, his arm wouldn't work.

All things considered, these trips are no big trick for the men. Guys like John Wayne show up in Vietnam with a three-day beard and nobody gets hurt but the Burma Shave people. But these gals really only have their glamor to sell and they sell, come hell or high water. Like in Korea, with a gale blowing and snow and sleet raising icicles on the trumpet section, these great gals took off their parkas and woolen scarfs to make their entrance in glamorous evening gowns. They managed it without turning blue, but when their performance was over, it took gallons of coffee and warm blankets to smooth out the goose pimples. While the trip is really worthwhile for what it does for the kids out there, it has one bonus for the performers—it can't help but change their lives in a way they never figured on.

You take Tuesday Weld, one of the outstanding rebels of all time. Tuesday didn't think she'd get anything out of the trip. She confessed to me that she doesn't really relate to strange people like we'd be meeting, but she gamely volunteered to go along anyhow. And for the first few days she was right. She'd do the show and she was great, and then she'd sort of climb back into her *Mad* magazine and she was somewhat removed from the people and things that were going on around her. But then something happened, and she was never the same girl again. I realized it when she was late making the plane in Tripoli and we were all standing there tapping our feet and she drove up and said she was sorry, but she was at the hospital. I asked her what was wrong and she said, "Nothing, I was just visiting the kids." I had to move her out of my kooky, irresponsible teen-ager file.

Charlton Heston did a man-size job in Vietnam for three weeks visiting remote outposts, answering questions, and also getting phone numbers so he could call the relatives of our service guys and assure them they were all in fighting condition.

Our SAG prez had some funny incidents while he was making these calls to the relatives, because it took him about five dollars' worth to convince them he was Charlton Heston. Very few people believe that Moses is still around.

One Marine in Danang hospital rocked him because when Chuck asked him for his phone number so he could call his wife the Marine said, "I'm not married."

Chuck said: "How about your mother and father?"

And the Marine answered: "They're both dead."

Heston said: "That hangs me up, doesn't it."

The Marine said: "No, would you give a message to the people back home?"

Chuck said: "I sure will."

"Well, tell all those Americans to get out of Berkeley."

Then there's Anna Maria Alberghetti, who went with us to Vietnam in '64. Her carefree, perhaps even self-centered attitude is best illustrated by an incident that occurred on our first takeoff. She climbed into the plane smoking a cigarette. What with gasoline fumes all over the place, one of the horrified crew gulped, "You shouldn't be smoking!" Anna Maria, touched by his concern, fixed him with a beautiful smile and said, "It's all right—I don't inhale." But a few days later at Subic Bay we couldn't get this girl to consider herself. She'd tripped over something and opened a nasty gash in her head, and the medics were prescribing a couple of days off, but she refused to miss one performance. And if you don't think that's brave, try to remember that she was working in front of Les Brown's band.

Moving a troupe the size of ours requires a certain amount of logistics, and the Air Force cooperates down to the minutest detail. For example, the night before we left, we were all issued special maps, indicating the place and time of our departure. The maps were drawn in so explicit and simple a fashion, the dizziest member of our cast couldn't help but follow it. Eight in the morning was our deadline and I had left a call for six-thirty because I wanted to set a good example by being on time. I was up bright-eyed and bushy-tailed, and after a quick breakfast, it was yoicks and away, my trusty map by my side. I might have broken a few speed laws in my attempt to be early, but it was worth it. I arrived at the landing field to discover that I actually was the first one to appear. The only difficulty being that I was at the wrong airport.

# CHAPTER TWO

It's amazing how many people will get up at the crack of dawn and come out to a cold airport just to cheer as I leave the country.

Among those present were members of the press, TV cameramen, military personnel, families and friends of the cast. An Air Force band from March Field blared away as we milled about, cheering us up no end with such encouraging numbers as "Praise the Lord and Pass the Ammunition" and "Coming in on a Wing and a Prayer."

The city fathers were represented by my friend, Supervisor Warren Dorn, who presented me with a huge Christmas card signed by the mayors of the seventy-six cities in Los Angeles County, which he asked me to "give to our boys over there."

An interesting incident occurred just prior to our takeoff. Fifty recruits were sworn into the Air Force to become "The Bob Hope Flight" at Lackland Air Force Training Base. Then a bronze trophy naming me "Honorary Air Force Recruiter" was handed to me, but as I reached for it, the plaque fell off the trophy. I looked at the plane and said, "I hope that's built better than *this*."

The trophy and the giant Christmas card were just two of the dozens of items handed to me. By the time I was ready to get on the plane, I looked like a war surplus store with legs.

The warmth and sincere good wishes of those who came to see us off gave us all a glow of satisfaction. Like Les

33

*Here we are on our way to the Far Eastern Camp Runamuck. (NBC Photo by Gary Null)*

White and Norman Sullivan, two of my collaborators, waving good-bye with one hand, and holding their skiis and golf clubs in the other. They were really happy to see me go.

Finally, all the pictures were taken, the interviews given, the farewells said, we trooped aboard the C-141 Star-Lifter, which was to be sort of home for us for the next twelve days.

The StarLifter is quite a plane. The Pentagon is very proud of it, and well they should be. It looks like the Pentagon with wings.

It can carry an incredible load, 94,000 pounds. Which worked out great. That's just about the weight of my idiot cards.

What a monster! It can carry an entire infantry company, or, to put it another way, it can get Jackie Gleason overseas in only two trips.

All the plane jokes that end with "—if they ever get it off the ground!" apply in spades to this baby. As Peter Leeds said after his first look at this mammoth aircraft, "I understand it has six engines and a truss!"

But large as it was, we really put this giant of cargo planes to the test.

In addition to our group of sixty-three and a crew of twelve, we also squeezed aboard tons of electrical and sound equipment, cameras, props, scenery, and all the paraphernalia that we knew from past experience we'd need to put on our shows overseas.

But to everyone's surprise, including the pilot's, the plane actually took off, and we were soon headed for our first stop, Wake Island, a mere twelve hours away.

A lot of people want to know the mechanics of putting a show like this together. The first and most urgent of the preparations is to check the availability of Dr. Freddie Miron. Dr. Miron is my therapist and the only one in the world who knows the combination for putting my bones together in the morning. And you think Oral Roberts is a miracle maker with the laying on of hands! Before we go any farther, and the suits for practicing medicine without a license start coming in, perhaps we should explain that the Doctor part of Freddie's title is honorary. We gave it to him like we did to Louis Shurr for service above and beyond the call of duty, out of affection, and because it gets them better seats on the airlines. Heaven only help some poor suddenly afflicted traveler who keels over and the cry goes up "Is there a doctor?" and a misguided stewardess says, "I believe one of the passengers is a Dr. Shurr."

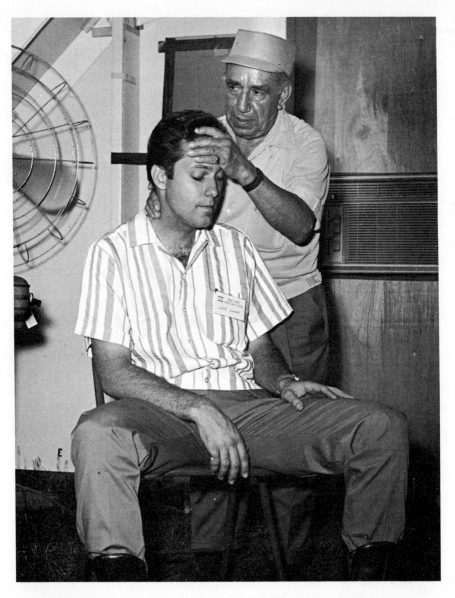

*"O, Lord, let this man sing again."* (NBC Photo by Gary Null)

Louis is not even a veterinarian, which Freddie could possibly get away with just on the basis of some of his dates. But I would no more think of going on a trip without Dr. Miron than I would of leaving without my caps and eyelash curler.

Once Dr. Miron's availability is established, we can go about planning the rest of the trip. Les Brown's band is no problem. They were born to it. You know—like some families sign up their babies at Groton or Harvard.

First, Les asks a prospective band member if he's willing to go to Vietnam, then he tells him to take music lessons. None of 'em ever listens, unfortunately.

But Les's band has one inescapable advantage—they fit together beautifully on the bus. No group of this type is ever complete without a Mother Superior, and this one's is Butch Stone.

Butch is the baritone sax man who sits right behind me when I do my monologues, so just slip through my Christmas shows and you can see him age right before your eyes. I don't understand it, because right while he's aging, I'm getting younger. Butch is really a mother hen, though, with the band. He wipes their noses, looks after their luggage, takes away their cigarettes, and hands out the sheet music. They do get music in spite of what your ears tell you. In addition to these chores, Butch sings a great song and does a show-stopping dance with Stumpy Brown each year on our Christmas Special. Surely you must have seen it. Butch is the one that gets kicked in the groin. That's what stops the show.

Another regular in the band is Geoff Clarkson, pianist and composer, and obviously a lot more than that, because what he brought back from one of our trips to the Orient was a bride—a stunning Nipponese named Yoriko, making idiots of the rest of the band who brought back transistors.

It's become a sort of tradition on these trips to kid about the plane, the pilots, and everything connected with the flight. And this trip was no exception. Our captain, Major

Kastner, and his great crew, laughed louder than anybody when we did lines such as these:

"We had a wonderful trip over, considering the plane MATS gave us. It took off from a kneeling position.

"It had every modern safety device . . . radar, sonar, automatic pilot, and curb feelers.

"But it's a beautiful plane, and now I know why they call it 'the flying boxcar.' Before we took off, they nailed the lid on.

"MATS gave us their most experienced pilot. He really has a lot of time in the air. He used to be a bartender at the Officers' Club.

"And I love the *esprit de corps* among the crew. The way they carried the pilot aboard . . . it took five of them . . . he fights!

"But it was inspiring to meet the crew . . . pilot, co-pilot, navigator, and chaplain.

"But I'm a little worried about our navigator. He got lost on the way to file our flight plan.

"I'm kidding, he was really good. After we'd been flying about five hours, he stuck his head in the cabin and said, 'What's all that water down there?' I said, 'That's the Pacific.' And he turned to the co-pilot and said, 'See? You owe me ten bucks!'

"But they're really great fliers, and I especially like the way they landed the plane . . . right side up!"

The flight was pleasant and uneventful till we got over Midway, where we did an impromptu radio show for the guys stationed there. Imagine doing a show at thirty-five thousand feet? It gives me a wonderful feeling of security working that far from the audience.

One by one, our cast went up front to the pilot's cabin and sent Christmas greetings to the men. Anita Bryant sang "Silent Night" in her inimitable fashion, Kaye Stevens and Jack Jones each did a number, and Colonna and I clowned around. Carroll Baker and Diana Lynn Batts just said "Hello" but that was plenty. The fellows down on

*The first time anyone whistled at her voice. (NBC Photo)*

Midway had never seen blips shaped like that on their radar before. Carroll summed it up very neatly with "Gee, that's the first time anybody ever whistled at my *voice!*"

There was one bit of unexpected drama during our broadcast. A plane, preparing to land on Midway, caught fire. We could hear the pilot's voice telling the control tower he was in trouble. In the excitement, Joey Heatherton got a little confused and thought it was our plane that was on fire. Poor girl! It took me two hours to calm her down. She finally broke my grip and went back to her seat.

We were happy to learn later that the pilot had landed safely.

One of the requisites for our show is a beautiful young dancer, and Mark Anthony, my Mafia agent, told me to watch a girl on one of Dean's shows. And I did. How lucky can you get? Joey Heatherton came on like nine and a half feet of wriggling teen-ager in a five-foot-four skin. She looked like she was trying to get outside of herself, which is ridiculous, because inside was where all the fun was. I couldn't wait to see what she'd do after she'd had her shots.

On this trip I took on an extra assignment I needed like Zsa Zsa Gabor needs a rhinestone. It happened this way. A few weeks before we left, I got a call from Charley McAdams, the boss at McNaughton Syndicate. He said, "Bob, you can do me a little favor on this trip." I said, "Anything, Charley, what do you need? A kimono for your wife? A used rickshaw? Autographed picture of Ho Chi Minh? Just name it."

He said, "Thanks, but that's not quite what I had in mind. I thought you could knock out a few columns for us while you're over there. You know . . . something funny with a human touch. The kind of thing you do so well."

As he said this, I got a flashback of last year's trip, the backbreaking schedule, the stifling heat, the gulped meals, the conditions of near-panic in which we worked, and the murderous pace, and said the only thing a sane man could say in reply to such an outrageous proposal. I said, "How many newspapers will carry the columns?"

He said, "Oh, about a hundred. It'll be read by about five or six million people, and the columns don't have to be long, just about three hundred words. You know what we want, Bob. A couple of belly laughs, a heart-tug or two, and a few pithy observations. Nothing to it, you can do it standing on your head."

I said, "Who snitched? I happen to do my best work in that position."

The idea of six million people eating my every word along with their Cheerios was too beautiful a vision to resist. The man in me overwhelmed the little judgment I had left, and I did what I always do when I'm faced with temptation. I gave in to it.

So the deed was done, the deal was made. Little did I know that the actual writing of the columns would be the easy part. Getting them transmitted to New York was another matter. I tangled with more red tape than Mao Tse-tung's tailor.

One thing that deluded me into thinking that doing the Vietnam columns would be a cinch was the fact that, some years ago, I'd turned out a daily column for the Hearst King Features Syndicate. And it was quite successful. In five years, there wasn't one complaint. Then somebody happened to read it!

As it turned out, my batting average with the Vietnam columns was surprisingly high. A few of them even made the front pages of newspapers all across the United States. A couple of them never got through at all. And one or two limped in a few days after I'd returned home.

But none of the columns could have gotten through without the perseverance, ingenuity, and persuasiveness of Bill Faith, a bright young public relations man who handled my press on this trip. Bill overcame language barriers, snags put in his path by arbitrary petty officials, begged, borrowed, or stole transportation when there wasn't any; in short, he overcame more obstacles than Batman in getting my deathless prose to my palpitating readers at home.

In fact, Bill was so great at handling hazards and smoothing things out where the going was rough, I'm no longer going to waste his talents in publicity. Starting Monday, he's going to caddy for me.

The first stop on our odyssey was Wake Island, the half-way point between Los Angeles and Bangkok. You all remember Wake Island? It was made famous during World War II by Warner Brothers.

Actually, Wake is a very strategic refueling base for our military aircraft. When we arrived, the bar was open, so the band refueled, too.

After being cramped in the plane for twelve hours, even Wake looked good to us, and that's saying a lot, because it's no Honolulu. In fact, it's not even Pasadena. It's sort of a runway with sharks. Wake consists of three tiny islands with a total area of about three square miles. On Wake, you don't take long walks unless you can swim.

I've been there a few times, and I think I know a thing or two about Wake. The island was discovered by Magellan while he was searching for the New World. He didn't even suspect it was there until he stubbed his toe on it. He took one good look at the island, threw all the Chianti overboard, and never again touched a drop.

Wake, surprisingly, has a nice little golf course. I wanted to play nine holes, but unfortunately the tide was in. Too bad, because it might have been fun. I've never had a barracuda for a caddy. The course really is short. It's the first time I've seen three one-par holes.

Originally, Wake was just a sanctuary for birds. The GIs stationed there say it's still for the birds.

We did a show for the island personnel in the airport building. Wake is so small we had to spread the audience around. If you put them all at one end, the whole island goes "Tilt!"

During the show, activity at the airport came to a complete halt. I don't know if any planes tried to land or take off during that time, but if they did, the only message they got from the control tower was, "Pick any runway you like, and good luck. This is a recording."

This non-sched show was also seen by a dozen or so very surprised people who were waiting for planes to various spots in the Pacific, and they were quite delighted to see a live show. One guy, headed for Hong Kong, looked at his plane ticket and said, "This is great! All they promised me was a movie!"

But doing the show on Wake benefited us as much as it pleased the audience. It gave us a chance to try out some of the new routines we'd been rehearsing. It was our version of breaking in a show out-of-town and believe me, you can't get much farther out of town than Wake Island. It's stuck there in mid-Pacific thirteen hundred miles from Guam and two thousand miles west of Hawaii. It's such a perfect location, I can't figure out how they missed it for a GI housing tract.

But all kidding aside, Wake is very important to us, and not only from a defense standpoint. It's also a great source of comfort to LBJ. It may one day come in handy as a place to send Senator Morse.

While we did the show, the plane was taking on gas . . . twenty-three thousand gallons of it. How about that? You buy twenty-three thousand gallons of gas and they don't even clean your windshield!

Our stint on Wake completed, we got back on the plane and took off on the last leg of the flight to Bangkok. Around this time, a little grumbling developed among some of the boys in the band and a few other malcontents.

*My monologue killed them everywhere. Obviously tickled pink is one of my writers, Charlie Lee; Trevor Armbrister of* The Saturday Evening Post; *and my PR man, Bill Faith.* (NBC Photo)

It seems they had passed up the TV dinner that had been served prior to our arrival at Wake, in the expectation of getting a more substantial meal on the island. Unfortunately, as so often happened when we hit a base, everything closed down so that all of the personnel could see the show, and on Wake, this included the kitchen staff.

And so, the thought of the tiresome ten-hour flight, with only the prospect of another TV dinner to sustain them, didn't bring out their better side. And when even the TV dinner was late, veiled threats of what I can only describe as mutiny began to be heard in various parts of the plane.

Butch Stone appointed himself the "Mr. Christian" of the semi-starved musicians and the other rebels and appealed directly to our resident troublemaker, Charlie Lee, who also poses as one of my writers. Charlie is a trencherman of note, and has the shape to prove it. A strong believer in direct action, Charlie said in a whisper they could hear all the way back in Honolulu, "We've waited long enough! Let's hijack the plane and fly it to a delicatessen!"

This did the trick. The mess officers sprung into action, and within four hours everyone aboard was reveling in a pre-cooked turkey dinner prepared by Maxim. Not "Maxim of Paris" . . . Maxim Kozak, the mess sergeant at Fort Dix!

GI chow has always been a fertile field for jokes with me. Soldiers have been griping about Army food since Pharaoh's legions, chasing Moses to the Red Sea, complained that the crocodileburgers were too tough. Of course, military life has improved in every way since then, but nevertheless, griping about the food goes on. It's as traditional as saluting, and I've taken advantage of it through several wars.

Surprisingly, few people know that the largest airline in the world is not Air France or Pan Am, but MATS, which flies our military to and from bases and installations all over the globe. They do a great job of flying, but because of limited facilities on their planes, they'll never rival the Brown Derby in the cuisine department. For that matter, they're no competition to Chicken Delight either.

On this subject, I've gotten some pretty large laughs from GIs with lines like these:

"This was the hundredth flight I've made across the Pacific and MATS made quite a ceremony of it. They bronzed my box lunch.

"And y'know something? It tasted better that way!

"I had a strange feeling I'd been on this plane before. I knew I was right when they gave me the same box lunch

45

I had in '62. My initials were still on the chicken leg right where I carved 'em.

"The Pentagon really went all out on this flight. They even showed a movie. It was very exciting. *Three Hundred Ways to Cook C Rations.*

"And the band came up with a great new game. They throw their box lunches overboard and watch the sharks get sick."

We landed at Don Muang Airport in Bangkok around midnight, bone-weary after twenty-two grueling hours in the plane. The predemonstration college students who used to get their kicks out of seeing how many of them could squeeze into a phone booth would know how we felt. The sound of our bones creaking as we stood up and stretched and staggered off the plane could have rivaled a Saturday night dance at Sun City.

Adding to our fatigue was the feeling of unreality that comes entering a different time zone. It was midnight in Bangkok, but only 9 A.M. in Los Angeles. It's a feeling you never quite get used to. During this trip, we went in and out of more time zones than a guy on LSD.

But that pooped feeling vanished when we saw the crowds waiting to greet us at the airport. There were more Klieg lights and photographers than I've seen at some of Hollywood's biggest premieres.

What a turnout! There were thousands of servicemen and Thai movie fans there. As Carroll Baker and the other girls stepped off the plane, there was a deafening roar. Then my blond wig fell off and they recognized me.

We were welcomed at the airport by General Richard Stilwell, who was head of all U.S. forces in Thailand, and Major Ed Swinney, project officer on several of our Christmas trips, who is now doing a great job running the Pacific edition of *Stars & Stripes.*

When we got to the Erawan Hotel where we'd stayed the previous year, there was another enthusiastic crowd of

*"Unfortunately they meant me, too."* (NBC Photo)

movie fans. I almost had my clothes torn off as I fought my way into the lobby. Serves me right for getting in front of Carroll Baker.

But we eventually got to our rooms and the long day finally ended. The last thing I remember was General Stilwell saying some of the sweetest words in the language to a golfer: "Don't forget, Bob, we tee off at nine-thirty."

I don't think I'll soon forget the nine holes of golf I played the following morning. General Stilwell and I were joined by Air Marshal Dawee Chulasap, who's the number three man in Thailand, and Major General Hiranyattitchi, who's also secretary of the Royal Bangkok Sports Club where we played.

I did all right with Air Marshal Dawee, but I didn't pronounce General Hiranyattitchi's full name because as I said, we only played nine holes. If you find these Thai names intriguing, here's one to play with on your portable. The reporter who interviewed me in Bangkok was Theh Chongkhadikij! Fortunately, he had no middle initial! Personally, I love those Thai names. They have a nice musical ring, and besides, they make a wonderful eye test. And if you say them real fast, you'll never again have to use dental floss.

But back to the game. The course at the Royal Bangkok Sports Club has one of the oddest layouts I've ever seen. The course is interspersed by a network of canals, or klongs, as they're called there. Lloyd Bridges would make a wonderful pro there. But it was interesting. It's the first time I've had a caddy with a snorkel. I ran into more trouble than Phyllis Diller at the "Miss America" contest. I hit so many canals, they began to call me "King Klong."

It was a typical Thai day, very hot and humid, but fortunately the Thais have several charming customs that help you survive. The caddy follows you around with an umbrella which he holds over your head. And on every hole, after you putt out, a guy slips a chair under you at the edge of the green and gives you a cold towel to wipe your head. Another attendant is always at your elbow with a Thermos of ice water. I haven't received that much attention since I walked into the maternity ward at Cedars of Lebanon by mistake!

As a sort of added attraction, the course borders on the Bangkok racetrack. I have a hunch they let the thoroughbreds graze on the links at night because the fairways are really lush. But I didn't have too good a day. Between the canals and the racetrack, I lost seventeen balls and four races.

The only thing on the schedule our first day in Bangkok was a rehearsal at 4 P.M., so everyone took advantage of the time off for sightseeing and shopping. And there's plenty to see in Bangkok, which is one of the most fascinating and colorful cities in the world. Centuries-old pagodas contrast sharply with office buildings as modern as any on Madison Avenue. Everywhere one sees the ancient and the new, side by side. It's not unusual to see pretty girls dressed in high fashion passing a kimono-clad native staggering under a heavy load balanced on a long pole.

Bangkok has a population of over two million, which is very surprising considering the traffic there. I've done a lot of jokes about Los Angeles traffic and the California freeways, but they're models of safety and efficiency compared to Bangkok where, it seems, all 2 million inhabitants are trying to beat the same traffic light.

The native name for Thailand is "Muang-Thai," which means "Land of the Free." And after seeing the traffic in Bangkok, I can tell you it's also the home of the brave! Talk about wild drivers! You can get a Purple Heart just crossing the street. Where else can you do sixty and be passed by a little old lady driving a pedicab? A pedicab is a vehicle with three wheels, two of which are entirely unnecessary.

It's the first time I've seen traffic cops praying. What

*How I retired on thirty dollars a month in Ta Khli. (NBC Photo by Gary Null)*

drivers! No one signals, traffic lights are ignored, and they have a very simple way of getting through a traffic jam. They just close their eyes and step on the gas. Bangkok's the only place in the world where brakes are optional equipment. I've seen cars bumper to bumper—but never three stories high. Now I know why Thailand has never been conquered. No invading army could get through that traffic.

But I was happy to learn that Bangkok is working on a plan that'll help solve the traffic problem. They're building one lane just for accidents.

I don't get much time for sightseeing, but I did manage to take in the klongs that crisscross Bangkok. They're like wet freeways and they're everywhere. In fact, you can get anywhere you want to go by water. And if you drink it, you'll get there twice as fast.

The main klong that winds through Bangkok is a world of its own. Thousands of families are born, live out their lives, and die there, without knowing any other kind of existence. Some live in crude shacks along its banks, others on boats, many of them the "do-it-yourself" variety.

The klong is the home of Bangkok's famed "Floating Market," which is quite a sight around 6 A.M. when the action reaches its peak. Hundreds of boats of all shapes and sizes somehow squeeze past each other loaded with fruit, vegetables, and other native foodstuffs which they sell to each other and to the people along the banks. It's something like L.A.'s Farmers Market during the rainy season.

The amazing thing is that many of these boats are propelled by wizened old ladies in their seventies. How they summon the strength for this backbreaking toil is something an outsider finds hard to understand, but they've been doing it longer than Crosby's been singing "White Christmas." I always remember this scene when Dolores comes home from a shopping trip and complains that she had to park half a block away from the supermarket.

Just the same, the klongs had some funny angles which turned up in my monologue. Such as:

"In Bangkok, people live on houseboats and are served by floating markets. You can just sit there and anything you want will float by . . . and a lot of things you don't.

"This whole place looks like someone forgot to replace the manhole cover.

"You have to be careful when you visit a girl who lives on one of the canals. If her husband comes home and the tide's against you, you've had it.

"I've never seen so many rivers and canals in my life. This morning I met the mayor . . . Charlie the Tuna.

"But these canals really come in handy. If you miss the bus, you can swim downtown."

Most of the troupe spent the afternoon shopping, and Bangkok, famed for its silk, its bronze tableware, exotic bric-a-brac, and beautifully wrought jewelry and precious stones, really brought out the bargain-hunting instincts in our nutty nomads. Traveler's checks clutched in their trembling hands, they swarmed over the city like a plague of locusts. Some headed for the PX, some to the "exclusive" shops they had been touted on by shills in the hotel.

When they got back to the Erawan for the rehearsal that afternoon, they were loaded down with the most incredible assortment of baubles, bangles, beads, and gewgaws I've ever seen. Flushed with excitement, they proudly displayed the loot they had "stolen" from the naïve local tradesmen. Things like temple bells, teak elephants, some of which were almost life-size, ivory back scratchers, bronze Buddhas, hand-carved umbrella stands, fighting fish, clawless otters . . . you know, all the things no home in California should be without.

Barney McNulty, whose skill at trading is attested to by the fact that he has two garages and no house . . . and whose shrewdness at haggling has been developed by countless forays into the marketplaces of the world, had really surpassed himself. He came back with a genuine imitation diamond bracelet, set in gleaming plastic, lovingly handmade by native craftsmen in Teaneck, New Jersey. He had cunningly tricked the storekeeper into letting this priceless gem slip through his fingers for a paltry eighty-three dollars!

What fools! If I say so myself, I'm proud of the restraint I show on these trips. It's not for nothing that I'm known by tradesmen throughout the Orient as "Hard-sell Hope." Before I leave on a trip, I make a list of what I need and I stick to it. I buy only those things that are absolutely necessary and practical. And this trip was no exception. All I came home with was eight hundred yards of Thai silk. It really is practical; at least it will be when Dolores is finished with it. It'll be the most beautiful pool cover in North Hollywood.

Diana Lynn Batts was the lone holdout in this buying spree. She refused to buy anything at all, and for a good reason. She resented the fact that in Bangkok they don't give Green Stamps.

Late that afternoon, in the banquet room of the Erawan Hotel, the cast assembled for what we loosely call a rehearsal. Also present was a horde of reporters, photographers, autograph hunters, a few curious tourists, and some hotel bellboys who watched the proceedings with monumental indifference.

The main purpose of this rehearsal was to try out the sketch we were going to do on the tour. I should explain here that in planning these Christmas trips, we keep our sketches as simple as possible, with a minimum of props, so that they can be done anywhere, at even the most remote bases, where stage facilities are at best makeshift, and often nonexistent.

For this tour, our scribes had cooked up a hospital sketch

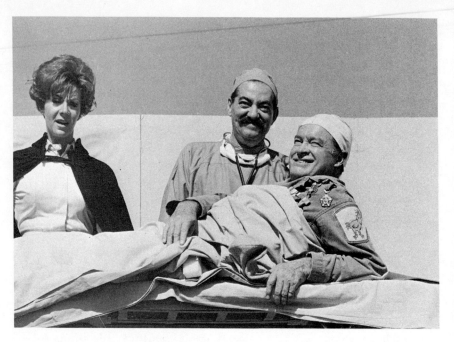

*I didn't mind but I was shot by* OUR *side.* (*Charles Moore © Curtis Publishing Co. 1966*)

which neatly filled all the requirements; it was not only simple, but funny. Professor Colonna played a mad Army surgeon. Everybody takes shots before they leave on tour— not me. I take Colonna. I'm superstitious about Jerry. He's sort of a good luck amulet I use to ward off rare diseases and evil spirits. And each year for twenty-five years I've had to *plead* with him to make the trip. The dialogue is always the same. Just before Christmas I call him and say, "Hello, Stash." And he says, "I'm packed."

In the sketch Kay Stevens played a very cynical GI nurse who went strictly by the book, with hilarious results. Butch

Stone, Stumpy Brown, Peter Leeds, and Jack Jones also were featured in the sketch and, as last-minute extras, we pressed into service Freddie Miron, my masseur, Bob Green, Anita Bryant's husband, and John Mathis, a college boy from Southern Methodist who was along to report the trip for his campus newspaper.

Freddie, Bob, and John did very well at this rehearsal. They got no laughs at all. So naturally I kept them in.

Stumpy Brown, Les's brother, who plays sax in the band, is an asset to any sketch. He projects well and has great timing. And he has one other thing in his favor, he looks funny. He's short and cute and enjoys our exploiting his lack of height. In this sketch, he played a GI who reports on sick call claiming he's suffering from a "rare tropical disease." When challenged by Nurse Stevens, who accuses him of goldbricking, he says, plaintively, "Honest, yesterday I was six feet tall!" Unmoved, Kaye says, "You sure you didn't jump without a chute?" and assigns him to germ warfare where he can become the head germ.

You may find this hard to believe, but my directors, especially Jack Shey, my TV director, have sometimes complained that I don't rehearse enough. To this ridiculous charge I've always had a ready answer. I explain that too much rehearsal dilutes the spontaneity of my performance. Not only that, rehearsals take me away from my regular business, which everyone knows is golf. Besides, our shows have been very successful through the years with our own particular *modus operandi* . . . that's Latin for "idiot cards."

As the TV viewing public knows by now, idiot cards are a necessity and very few shows can do without them. On our show they're especially important because we make changes up to the very last minute, polishing lines or adding a joke on a news item that's just broken and calls for comment.

Another reason cue cards are so important is that big-

*Some guys won't settle for just an autograph. (NBC Photo by Gary Null)*

name guest stars with their tight schedules simply don't have the time for long rehearsals. Frank Sinatra, for instance, will give you at most an hour. Which is quite a sacrifice considering what he has to go home to.

Dean Martin's another guy who doesn't think much of rehearsing. But despite this carefree attitude, Dino's got one of the most successful variety shows in television. Which is quite an accomplishment when you consider that he can't even see the idiot cards.

Another famous rehearsal-dodger is Jackie Gleason. But Jackie can get away with it, because he has one of the most fantastic memories in show business. He can scan an entire script once and remember every word. Of course, the fact that Jackie's talent is as big as he is doesn't hurt.

But to get back to the rehearsal that afternoon, despite the picture-taking and other interruptions, we did manage to get the sketch in good-enough shape for our first show, scheduled for the following morning. This was in no small part due to the fact that Colonna and Kaye Stevens have voices that can be heard over a Beatles' concert. Compared to them, Ethel Merman is Whispering Jack Smith.

That evening, a few of the more adventurous spirits among us took in some Thai boxing matches. Boxing in Thailand is completely different from ours. Over there, the hands are rarely used. The referee says, "All right, shake feet and come out fighting." The fighters then face each other in the center of the ring and start kicking field goals in each other's teeth. It's like a stockholders' meeting at NBC. And all through the bout, music is played and the fighters hit in rhythm to the music. This phase of Thai boxing isn't too different from ours. I've seen many a fifteen-round waltz over here.

But in Thailand the feet are all-important, so each boxer has a second and a chiropodist. And for the big championship fights, they have a choreographer.

The really amazing thing about Thai boxers is that their faces are never scarred or disfigured. That's because in Thai boxing the idea is to go after the body, and thus the face remains unmarked. However, body blows do plenty of damage. Thailand is the only place in the world where boxers wind up with cauliflower navels.

The roughness of Thai boxing is a paradox, as is cockfighting, which is also popular, because the Thais are fundamentally a gentle, soft-spoken people. They regard the mere raising of one's voice as barbaric. Imagine, no screaming or hollering! Now you know why Leo Durocher's never been to Thailand.

57

# CHAPTER THREE

Around nine the next morning, we landed in a C-130 at Udon for our first scheduled show of the tour. Udon is the site of an American air base located close to the border of Laos in really primitive Thai hinterland. It might be described as "Hertz Rent A Water Buffalo" country. It's a rather desolate area, arid and flat and sparsely inhabited.

The housing consists mainly of huts, hootches, and palm-covered barracks. The audience numbered about twenty-five hundred, three hundred of whom were from a nearby base at Nakhon Phanom, which the GIs quickly renamed "Naked Fanny."

The stage was in the middle of the ball park and had been built on a sea of drums containing high-octane aviation fuel. Smokey the Bear would have been horrified. And I was a little nervous myself. I couldn't help thinking—one carelessly tossed cigarette and we might all wind up as astronauts. But fortunately nothing happened. Even Joey Heatherton's torrid dance didn't start a blaze, although I noticed that even the GIs without cigarettes were smoking.

Another hazard at Udon was the proximity of the Viet Cong, many of whom had taken refuge in nearby Laos, and had infiltrated the area. I have a hunch a few "Charleys" may have sneaked into the audience. During my monologue, I spotted one strange-looking guy taking notes. That in itself is not unusual, but this fellow was in a tree. Right now he's probably doing my act in Loew's Hanoi. Oh, well, that's show business. Besides, the new comedians have to come from someplace.

*"In case of a raid head right for my dressing room."* (*NBC Photo by Gary Null*)

During the show, flights of jets streaked over the base and it seemed to me that the audience was unduly interested in watching them. Why did they keep looking up at these jets, I wondered. They see them all the time. I found out later that the guys weren't just watching. They were counting.

If they saw a flight of four jets, or two, they relaxed. But if there were only three planes, or just one, that meant that one of them had not made it back from a mission over North Vietnam. That was how the chilling reality of the war was brought home to us at our very first show.

This hit us even harder in the middle of the show. Kaye Stevens had just finished her number when I noticed a stir in the audience. Then I saw a pilot being carried in and placed on a truck in front of the stage. I didn't know what to make of it until an officer rushed up and whispered to me that this pilot had been shot down only two hours ago. He had managed to bail out but landed in a tree in the jungle, a few yards from a platoon of Viet Cong. Our fighter planes had circled the area keeping the Cong at bay until a helicopter had dropped a sling and pulled him out.

His name was Jim Sullivan. His face looked pasty-white and he was obviously in shock. The doctors thought it would be good therapy for him to see the show. Imagine anyone thinking my jokes could make someone well? Usually it's the other way around.

I got Captain Sullivan up on stage and interviewed him, drawing him out on some of the details of his ordeal. Needless to say, it wasn't quite as funny as the rest of the show, but it got a tremendous response from the guys, and to me, it was unforgettable.

After a hurried lunch, we got back on our C-130 and took off for Ta Khli and our second show of the day.

That pattern of two shows a day was followed almost throughout the entire tour. Two a day in that searing heat and strength-sapping humidity was tough on everyone, but the gals were out there—looking cool and beautiful every show because they felt we owed it not only to the GIs, but also to their families back home. We know it was well worthwhile because we received an avalanche of letters from grateful parents who had caught glimpses of their sons in the audience shots when our show was on the air in January. Those warm letters really got to me. They're the kind of "residuals" I like.

Ta Khli is one of the biggest U.S. bases in Thailand and is located in the heart of what is known as "King Cobra"

*This is Captain Jim Sullivan, who was shot down two hours before our show and rescued in time for the monologue. He doesn't look much worse for wear from either. (NBC Photo by Gary Null)*

country. The GIs there call it a "rest and recreation area for snakes." They also have other, more colorful names for it, which I can't mention here because I want this book to be read in Boston.

For you herpetologists (a word I picked up from "Zoo Parade"), the deadliest of all the snakes in that area is known as "Russell's Viper." The guys there call it a "three-stepper," because that's all you can take after it bites you.

That's why they don't have a golf course there. If you were to reach for your three-iron, you'd have to make darn sure it didn't reach for you first!

Fortunately, I didn't run into any snakes there, although some of the guys in the band swear they saw some. That, however, doesn't mean much. Les's boys see snakes even when they're in Burbank . . . in living color yet.

I hope you realize I'm kidding. I've done endless jokes about Les and the band, but they know I have the greatest respect and admiration for them. They have it rougher on these trips than any of us, and this was especially true of our last two treks to Southeast Asia.

One of the things that makes life tough in that part of the world is the never-ending heat and humidity. Kipling wasn't joshing when he said the sun comes up like thunder. It really beats down mercilessly from dawn to dusk.

The other performers and I are on stage only part of the time and can take refuge from the sun between our turns. But the band enjoys no breaks. The musicians are exposed to the murderous heat for two to three hours at a stretch and really take a beating. Temperatures in Thailand and Vietnam stay around a hundred, with humidity to match. By the end of our first day in Thailand, the band had been pretty well barbecued. Trumpeter Don Smith was one of the first casualties. His lips were so burned and swollen by the sun that he couldn't play for several days. In fact, all the guys in the band were so badly sunburned, they developed skin poisoning. But none of them complained.

As Butch Stone explained, "After all, when we realize that some of those kids had been sitting out there for eight and ten hours waiting for the show, a little sunburn doesn't seem worth mentioning."

The heat and humidity created another problem for the band. It put the instruments out of tune. This isn't too important when they're playing for dancers, but when they're accompanying a singer, it can really make a difference.

But the GIs over there are the ones who have to live and fight in that awful, debilitating heat. That's why one of the lines I did always got such a great response. It was . . .

"Incidentally, I have a message for you from your folks back home . . . 'Stay warm!'"

At Ta Khli, as at every other remote place we played, the GIs really extended themselves to provide the girls with little conveniences to make their stay more pleasant. Sometimes it was an electric fan set up in the tent that often served as a dressing room. Or lights strung around a mirror to help the girls with their makeup. At Ta Khli, they gave the girls huge native straw hats which are very effective in warding off the scorching sun. And the GIs solved another little problem with typical American ingenuity. The "powder" room was about half a mile away from the girls' dressing room, so they set up a rickshaw service to take the girls back and forth.

Carroll Baker got one of the bigger laughs of the day when she took a look at the rickshaw and said, "What a way to go!"

Because we were a little late in getting started, the show at Ta Khli lasted until well after dark. It was an interesting experience trying to read the idiot cards by the touch system. Now I know why New York's former mayor, Robert Wagner, didn't get any laughs during the big blackout.

But the darkness was not really a handicap. Dolls like Carroll Baker, Joey Heatherton, Diana Lynn Batts, Kaye

*Two tough Ta Khli warriors. I don't know who the guys in uniform are. (NBC Photo by Gary Null)*

Stevens, and Anita Bryant light up any stage better than Con Edison ever could.

Back in Bangkok later that evening, we went to a party hosted by General Stilwell at the Royal Sports Club. The entertainment was provided by a local Thai orchestra who played on instruments made of bamboo. Their style was very interesting. They shook and rattled the bamboo to create different notes. The effect was weird. I haven't heard a sound like that since Sonny and Cher backed into their electric guitar.

But Les and the boys got a big kick out of their Thai counterparts and their bamboo axes. They couldn't resist ribbing them, asking such questions as, "Who does your arrangements, Woody Herman?" and, "How often do you have your instruments treated for termites?"

Actually, though, once your ear got accustomed to it, the music was rather pleasant. All it took was a little patience and understanding and I've got lots of that. How else could I have survived all those years with Bing?

The following morning we were off to Ubon, an air base about 225 miles north of Bangkok, and forty-five miles from the Mekong River, which forms the border with Laos. In addition to our airmen, Ubon has a contingent of the Royal Australian Air Force. The Aussies and New Zealanders are among the few SEATO nations who have sent fighting men to Vietnam. The Aussies have a well-earned reputation as courageous and formidable warriors, and I'm sure glad they're on our side. They're tough, fearless, resourceful, and have great national pride. Evidences of this were all over the base. Everywhere you looked, they'd drawn, scrawled, or stamped their national insignia, the kangaroo. I think some of them even had kangaroos tattooed on them. Ubon is the only place in Southeast Asia where kangaroos outnumber the Coca-Cola signs.

Everywhere on these trips we'd pick up little nuggets of information about the local customs, which often come in handy in planning a show for a particular spot. En route to Ubon, for instance, we learned that it's quite common for the men in that region to stroll down the street holding hands.

Small world, isn't it. Whoever thought that places as far apart as Ubon, Thailand, and Hollywood Boulevard, California, would have the same quaint customs?

Another bit of news I got on the way to Ubon was that a couple of my vintage films had just been shown at the base, *Iron Petticoat* and *Paris Holiday*, neither of which had been contenders in the Oscar Derby. As a matter of fact, they'd both been nominated for the "Late Show" . . . before they were released. So, just as a safety measure, I made sure that in getting off the plane I was behind the big, broad, six-foot-four frame of Peter Leeds.

However, my fears were groundless. I got my standard reception. I was completely ignored as the guys rushed forward to greet Carroll Baker, Joey Heatherton, and the rest of the gals.

Why I'd wanna take another comic along when I'm there, I can't imagine, but Kaye Stevens turned out to be much more than a comedienne. In addition to great looks and personality, she has warmth—just what we needed in the steamy jungle. Kaye had a way of working that just wrapped those guys around her little finger which, given a choice, would certainly have not been their target. But the guys loved her and so did I, because with all the inconveniences, she was the only one who offered to share her hairdresser with me.

That girl killed me the first time I saw her. . . . It was at the Cocoanut Grove and she had just taken the place apart with her "Take Me Out to the Ball Game" specialty. The Frug Dancers followed her on and I was sitting there sipping my prune juice and trying to figure out a way to lasso this great talent, when I felt a tug at my arm and somebody said, "Pssst!" I looked down and it was Kaye on

*Hertz will rent you anything. (NBC Photo by Frank Carroll)*

her hands and knees—she had crawled down the aisle because she didn't want to destroy the mood the Fruggers had created on stage. She whispered, "How about taking me to Vietnam with you, Bob?" How about that? I was so stunned, I left without tipping the waiter.

At Ubon, the Nicholas Brothers ran into a cousin with the unlikely name of Ulysses Mosley, from Pensacola, Florida, who's a Specialist 5 with the Army. They had a pleasant reunion.

I didn't meet any relatives on this trip, which was just as well. I never carry more than twenty-five dollars in cash. And most of my relatives are the suspicious kind. They won't take checks.

Then we were off to Khorat, just a few minutes as the C-130 flies from Ubon. The actual name of the base at Khorat is Camp Usarthai.

At Khorat, the audience of about forty-two hundred consisted of U. S. Army, Navy, and Air Force and invited guests from the Royal Thai Army and Air Force, a few local Government officials, and several members of the Peace Corps. In addition, we also played to a herd of elephants and water buffalo who were grazing very close to the stage.

It developed into quite a staring contest. I didn't expect any reaction from the water buffalo, but I thought the elephants might perk up when I did some jokes kidding the Democrats. But nothing happened. I could only assume that these Thai elephants didn't want to get involved in politics for fear of jeopardizing their foreign aid.

Besides being one of our more important bases in Thailand, Camp Usarthai has another distinction. It's close to the town of Khorat, which offers a variety of diversions to the GIs off duty; dance halls, nightclubs, bars, and other attractions designed to make the weary GI forget the war for an hour or two. To put it another way, it's sort of a

Disneyland for adults. And if you're not an adult when you get there, you are after you leave.

We'd been briefed on this play area and so came prepared with appropriate comments, such as these:

"Here we are at Khorat . . . famous as the place where Suzie Wong got her basic training.

"It's nice to be here at this Far Eastern Camp Runamuck.

"I love the architecture here . . . everything is shaped like a pagoda . . . but enough about my date last night.

"At the nightclubs it costs two dollars an hour if you want someone to sit with you. I don't know how those girls can afford you fellows!

"The local drink here is called Anak. It's the first time I've seen rocket fuel in fifths.

"It's a great drink. It's such fun to take a sip . . . then sit there and watch your dog tags dissolve.

"It's quite a drink . . . it not only gives you a lift, it also kills crabgrass, whether you have any or not.

"Now I know what happened to Yul Brynner's hair." And so on. I'm sure you get the idea.

I'll always remember Khorat because during our show something happened that could have ended the tour for me right there. I was standing backstage waiting to go on, when someone accidentally bumped into me. I lost my balance and fell backward off the stage.

At panicky moments like that, your whole life is supposed to flash before you. That didn't happen to me. All *I* saw was a nightmarish vision of Peter Leeds getting tremendous laughs with my monologue. And even worse, I saw Jack Jones putting his arms around Carroll Baker as they did *our* duet.

But the lucky monkey's paw I'd bought from that fortune teller in Bangkok must have been working because my fall was broken by Robert Raft, a security man, who just happened to be standing there. If it weren't for him, I might have fallen on my nose and had to quit show business. As it was, I tore a couple of ligaments in my left ankle, though I didn't know it then.

The incident seemed very unimportant and I was honestly surprised when the press made quite a thing of it. It even made headlines in a lot of papers back home. It was all a little embarrassing. I never dreamed a couple of my ligaments would be almost as newsworthy as LBJ's gall bladder.

It was also embarrassing on another count. Although the injury wasn't disabling, it was painful when I put my weight on the foot, so I limped around for a few days, which made me feel downright silly. Picture the scene. Here I was among guys who put their lives on the line every day, and battle casualties who had been brought out to see the show in wheelchairs and who felt themselves fortunate just to be there. And there I was limping around the stage with my piddling disability, caused by an idiotic fall. I felt like a guy who shows up at the Indianapolis 500 with a pogo stick!

This had happened to me once before, in '43 in North Africa.

It was in Bizerte, and we were returning to headquarters in a GI truck when the air raid sirens came on. Someone yelled "Hit the ditch!" so we all jumped out and lay face down in a ditch by the side of the road.

I lay there for several minutes until it became apparent that there were no enemy planes anywhere near us. But when I tried to get up, I felt a sharp twinge in my left hip. To my chagrin, I had to be helped to my feet and then lifted back onto the truck. The payoff was that I had to walk with a cane for a week, but the real injury was to my pride. It's tough to have to explain that you got wounded hiding.

When we got back to Bangkok an old friend from our original U.S.O. trip to Alaska, Colonel Bob "Growing Pains" Gates, met us and had his friend, Arthur B. Tarrow, the head of the hospital at Clark Field who happened to be on business in Bangkok, tape my ankle. He told me to stay off it as much as possible for the next few days. This put a crimp in our routine because there were two spots in the show where I was called upon to display my terpsichorean brilliance. One was a dance bit with the Nicholas Brothers which ended in a fast "challenge routine." And I had also been doing a parody on "Will You Still Be Mine?" with Carroll Baker, which we finished with a combination tap and soft shoe number.

So for the next two or three shows, I had to cut out my dancing, which was not only frustrating to me but also a great loss to the countless lovers of the dance in our audiences.

This may not be generally known, but dancing has always been close to my heart. In fact, that's how I got my first laugh on a stage. My style of dancing has always been unique and that's because I never had any formal training. I developed this style as a kid on the sidewalks of Cleveland—picking up pennies with my toes. I wish I'd known some of those pennies were hot. I still have "E Pluribus Unum" clearly engraved on my big toe.

Sometimes I regret not having put more emphasis on my dancing. Who knows? I might've been a Senator from California.

However, I managed to limp through the show at Khorat although every so often someone would notice me hopping around and say, "Where's Marshal Dillon?"

Fortunately, my ankle wasn't too painful to prevent me from attending the party being given for us that night by Their Majesties, King Bhumibol and Queen Sirikit, which, as in the previous year, was the highlight of our visit to Thailand.

Getting invited to the royal palace is a great honor in Thailand and an enormous boost to one's social standing. When the invitations were delivered to the hotel, a remark-

*Funny, the water didn't affect* HER. (*NBC Photo by Gary Null*)

able change took place in the attitude of the personnel. We were no longer just a bunch of itinerant actors but were transformed into instant VIPs.

This rise in our social status became evident in many ways. The maids now knocked before they entered my room. When I ordered breakfast, it was delivered that same morning. The phone service suddenly became a model of efficiency. When I made a call, I got through with only three wrong numbers. The bellhops became very solicitous and one even asked me for my autograph. After I'd given it to him, he looked at me in awe and said, "I hear you very big Hollywood movie star. Tell me, you know Keye Luke?" Such is fame.

But most miraculous of all, the air conditioning in my room, which had been dormant ever since my arrival, suddenly whirred into action with such force that within twenty minutes I looked like Nanook of the North.

The invitation to the royal shindig, with its attendant inflation of the ego, affected others in our gang of gadabouts. For instance, Barney McNulty, custodian of our idiot cards, bestowed a new title on himself as "Grand Vizier of the Visual Aids."

John Pawlek, our sound man, became "Director of Decibel Control."

Joan Maas, our capable production assistant, decided on "Maharanee of Rewrites."

And Mike Moschella, my makeup man, settled on a title he'd been toying with ever since he started working on me: "Master of the Miracle."

I couldn't help thinking that all this was in sharp contrast to a previous encounter with royalty back in 1958, on another Christmas tour. We'd gone to Rabat, the capital of Morocco, for an audience with King Mohammed who, we'd been assured, was most anxious to meet me and the rest of the troupe. However, somebody must have goofed, because when we arrived at the palace and I identified myself, the guard said, "Bob *who?*"

This was a little frustrating, but I figured this guy would see reason as soon as he realized how important I really was, so I tried again. I said, "I'm Bob Hope . . . you remember . . . star of *The Road to Morocco*," and waited for a reaction. It came quickly. I heard a click and realized he'd released the safety catch on his rifle. Having a highly developed sense of self-preservation, I tried a new tack, which had always worked pretty well for me in breaking down barriers . . . name-dropping. I said, "One of my dearest friends is Danny Thomas." This got me nothing but a cold stare. In desperation, I rattled off such names as Pepe le Moko, Turhan Bey, Little Egypt, Abou Ben Adhem, and Abdullah Bul Bul Amir. Nothing! It got about as much reaction as Annette Funicello at the Berkshire Music Festival.

I left quietly, mumbling something under my breath about cutting off their foreign aid.

But back to Bangkok and current triumphs. Those of us who'd been to the palace the year before briefed the newcomers on how to behave in the royal presence and on protocol in general.

Every country has its customs, rules, taboos, do's and don'ts, a virtually endless list of things to trip the unwary tourist. The countries of Southeast Asia are especially touchy about any infraction of what they consider good taste or courtesy.

For instance, in Thailand, you must remove your shoes before entering a temple, and men's arms and women's shoulders must be covered. Shaking a finger at someone, crossing your legs so that your foot points at someone, and placing one's hand on the head or shoulders of another is considered very bad form, if not an affront. You have to be more careful than a tattoo artist in a nudist colony.

It's quite a responsibility and really puts you on your best behavior. In some parts of the world not as friendly as Thailand you practically have to walk a tightrope because one wrong word or gesture can trigger a riot. That explains why in these supersensitive areas, when a tourist asks for the American Embassy, a native points to a pile of ashes.

Pride in one's country and its mores is perfectly laudable and understandable. However, sometimes some petty official becomes so touchy on the subject that he sees a slight in a perfectly innocent gesture or statement and what the newspapers call "an incident" is created. A good example of this was the recent war between Mexico and Frank Sinatra over a characterization in Frank's movie, *Marriage on the Rocks*, which was interpreted by the Mexican Government as insulting.

In retaliation, Mexico barred all of Frank's movies from being shown, placed an embargo on his records, and declared him *persona non grata* in that country.

In the excitement, no one remembered that Frank, not long before, had done a benefit for underprivileged Mexican kids, or the world tour Sinatra had made for a similar cause a few years earlier.

Of course, I couldn't let a topic like this go by without making a few comments about it on my TV show. As I recall, I said:

"How about Sinatra being barred from Mexico? Dean Martin got so mad, he stopped using tequila for a chaser. Imagine Mexico barring a guy just because of a few lines in a movie? That's what I call Tijuana brass! So far, Frankie's been very nice about it. But wait till Trini Lopez tries to play Las Vegas. Mexico may be in big trouble. Frankie just issued green berets to Joey Bishop, Peter Lawford, and Sammy Davis!"

These quips got big laughs everywhere except in Mexico.

The show had barely faded from the tube when a protest was forthcoming from the Mexican Consulate in Los

Angeles, and I became Public Enemy Number Two in Mexico, right behind Sinatra.

Fortunately, this bit of unpleasantness blew over quickly, for which I was grateful. I've always enjoyed my visits to Mexico and admired their people. In fact, I saw *Viva Zapata!* seven times, and I still have a guitar pic autographed by Tito Guizar that I cherish.

But try as you may, you can't help offending someone. The British still haven't quite forgiven me for a joke I did about Princess Margaret. They were really miffed. In fact, for a few years after that incident, I had to sneak into England under the name of Danny Kaye. Which worked fine until my blond wig fell off.

Needless to say, we were all thrilled at the prospect of meeting the King and Queen of Thailand, and somewhat in awe because we were keenly aware of the reverence in which the King is held. To give you an idea, his full title is: "His Majesty The Supreme Divine Lord, Great Strength of the Land, Incomparable Might, Greatest in the Realm, Lord Rama, Holder of the Kingdom, Chief of the Sovereign People, Sovereign of Siam, Supreme Protector and Monarch."

Quite a title, isn't it? I'm surprised DeGaulle didn't think of it first.

King Bhumibol has a most unusual background. He was born in 1927 in Cambridge, Massachusetts, the first king ever to be born in the United States. At the time, his father, Prince Mahidol, was a student at Harvard. His father died suddenly when Bhumibol was just two years old and he was taken back to Bangkok by his mother. He was educated in France and Switzerland, where he developed his enthusiasm for American jazz. He assumed the throne in 1946, following the mysterious death of his older brother, Ananda. He was only nineteen, one of the first teen-age kings in history.

Bhumibol demonstrated quickly that he would be no mere figurehead. He participated actively in the shaping of

*Our royalty, Miss USA, meets the real ones in Thailand. (NBC Photo by Gary Null)*

his country's development, and was instrumental in making Thailand one of the most stable and prosperous nations in Southeast Asia.

Thailand is our stanchest ally in Southeast Asia and has openly thrown in its lot with us despite the constant threats and provocations from Red China. This is due in no small part to the influence of the King, whose admiration for Americans and all things American is well known.

Unlike the traditional royal marriages in that part of the world, which are arranged long in advance by the parents, the union of King Bhumibol and beautiful Queen Sirikit was a true love match. It began in Switzerland when they were teen-agers and, unlike past kings, his great love for his wife was such that he renounced polygamy, for centuries the traditional prerogative of Thai royalty.

In Dubuque, Chillicothe, or Wichita having one wife may not come as astounding news but in Thailand, it's almost as unusual as it is in Hollywood.

Of course, Queen Sirikit is one of the great beauties of Thailand, a land noted for its lovely women. Her position precludes her entering a beauty contest. It's a shame, in a way. She could easily be "Miss Universe."

The royal palace is an impressive complex of buildings in the heart of Bangkok, completely surrounded by a ten-foot wall. It's quite a sight; it looks like a housing project in Texas.

The interior was just as impressive as we had anticipated, with all the opulence and splendor that one expects to find in a royal palace. The red carpet was so thick, Stumpy Brown stepped into the room and disappeared.

We entered through a long hallway and proceeded to the reception room where a protocol officer introduced us, each in turn, to the King and Queen seated in the center.

The King and Queen seemed genuinely delighted to see us. He said, "Mr. Hope, it is indeed a pleasure to have you back in our country." He smiled as he said this. He's a great diplomat.

I was proud of the way the troupe conducted themselves while being presented to Their Majesties. There wasn't a single *faux pas*, although Diana Lynn Batts carried informality a bit far when she acknowledged the King's greeting with an airy "Hi." But I suppose it was excusable. After all, her title of "Miss U.S.A." makes her a member of American "royalty" of a sort.

I was also pleasantly surprised at the aplomb with which Charlie Lee, never the soul of discretion, carried off his meeting with the royal couple. Upon being introduced, he

*The Queen of Thailand and the NBC peacock. (NBC Photo by Frank Carroll)*

not only said the right things, he even attempted a little curtsy. This may not sound like much but it was quite a feat for Charlie, who happens to be built like Toots Shor, but without Toots' sunny personality.

In addition to the King and Queen, also present were other members of the royal family, high-ranking military officials, society leaders, captains of industry, in short, the top echelons of Thai society.

Everyone was dressed to the nines. The women made a dazzling picture in their flowing, graceful saris, bedecked with brilliant gems, star sapphires, jades and rubies. I haven't seen anything like it since Zsa Zsa's last wedding reception.

Our gals were not outshone even in this brilliant assemblage. Carroll Baker was resplendent in a silver-beaded turquoise gown with the bottom half trimmed in ostrich feathers, which had been designed especially for her by Balmain, who, coincidentally, is also the favorite designer of Queen Sirikit. Carroll's gown had one other claim to attention: it was semi-transparent. She thought the Court might enjoy seeing her in it. They *did*.

For you gourmets, the dinner was a tasteful blend of Occidental and exotic Oriental dishes, most of which were curried or otherwise highly spiced with all sorts of condiments. The Thai brand of curry is really hot. I took a mouthful and was surprised to find it had a metallic taste. Then it hit me: my bridgework was melting. But I bravely took a few more mouthfuls of the fiery stuff. Then I sat back, relaxed, and calmly watched the smoke rings rising from my navel.

For me, one of the big thrills of the evening was being seated next to Queen Sirikit during dinner. I don't usually have any trouble keeping up my end of the conversation, but I must admit that this proximity to the enchanting, fairy-tale Queen slowed down the flow of *bon mots* and casual ad libs which have made me celebrated as the Noel

Coward of the Chicken Delight set. Come to think of it, what do you say to a queen during a three-hour dinner? The usual things don't quite fit. Things like "How's your old man making out at the factory?" or "What'cha think of last night's episode of 'Peyton Place'?" or "Do you think Sandy Koufax will win thirty this year?"

But fortunately the Queen sensed my predicament and graciously drew me out on the subject dearest to my heart —*me!* She asked me about my ankle, the trip from the States, the others in the troupe, and put me so much at ease that soon we were chatting away like old friends.

During our *tête-à-tête,* I learned some fascinating bits of information about the Queen and the palace, which may be of interest to distaff readers. For instance, the Queen flies her hairdresser in from Paris for special state occasions. I don't know who her hairdresser is, but he'd better be good. One pincurl out of place and he'd go home in the five o'clock cobra!

The Queen also supervises the four hundred servants it takes to run the palace. And I think more than half of them were working at the reception and dinner that evening. It really made for great service. It's the first time I've had eight liveried waiters serve me one anchovy.

After dinner we put on a short show which was highlighted by Anita's singing of "Battle Hymn of the Republic." This song may seem a little inappropriate for an audience in Thailand but they fully appreciated its universal theme and the grandeur of its message. They gave Anita quite an ovation. I did a few jokes and thanked the Queen and King for their gracious hospitality and their kindness to us.

After the show, Les Brown and the boys played for dancing. The King and Les have one thing in common: they're both amateur musicians. King Bhumibol is a jazz buff and also a composer. He must be pretty good. One of his melodies was included in the late Mike Todd's *Peep Show,* which played on Broadway in 1950.

*The King and Queen of Thailand. The King is being made an honorary musician by an honorary musician. (NBC Photo by Gary Null)*

The King also blows a swinging saxophone. It was made for him in the U.S.A. by Selmer and it's a little from the ordinary in one respect. It's made of solid gold. The King is very careful about his sax. He won't let anyone touch it. He unpacks it and packs it himself.

During our previous visit, the King told Les that he was especially fond of "Days of Wine and Roses," so, soon after getting home, Les had sent him a special arrangement of that number. The King had been practicing it all year and when we arrived, he was really ready. All through the show the King was waiting anxiously, his saxophone poised, for his cue to do his big number with the band.

But Les, true to form, completely forgot about this and sailed blithely through the number without as much as a glance at the frustrated monarch. However, being a king carries as much weight as being a member of the Musicians' Union, at least in Thailand. Showing himself to be a man of compassion and mercy, the King did not have Les beheaded. He merely suggested that the band play the number again, this time with him playing the lead sax. The inclusion of the King in the band made quite a difference. In fact, it had an entirely new sound . . . music!

The King was so pleased with his performance and was having so much fun that he suggested a jam session. Les said, "We'd love to, Your Majesty, but we have to be up at seven in order to fly out." Whereupon the King replied, "Great! We can play till seven, then you won't have to bother getting up!"

There's quite a bit of Frankie in the King.

Tired as they were, Les and the boys acceded to the King's suggestion. I suspect that the crocodile-filled moat they had to cross on the way out helped them make up their minds.

We all gathered around to enjoy the impromptu musicale, and I must say that the King winged it with all the virtuosity of a Downbeat Award winner. If he ever decides to start his own band, I know he'd do very well. I can see his billing now: "King Bhumibol and His Siamese Cats . . . The Swingin'est Music This Side of Cambodia!"

The session continued far into the night. It got pretty noisy but for some reason, the neighbors never complained.

It was a wonderful finish to a memorable evening.

The following day we did a show at Bangkok's Don Muang Airport for an audience of five thousand, consisting of airport personnel, Army people, diplomats, and Thais of every rank. We did our regular show, but news of my mishap had gotten around, so we added a few jokes on this topic to the monologue.

This has been standard procedure with us through the years: to comment on anything newsworthy almost instantaneously. Fortunately, my writers work best under pressure and are capable of what we in our organization call "instant brilliance." And they do this of their own free will. It's not true that I carry a golf club at all times to stimulate their thinking. Thus, my bad ankle brought forth such gems as these:

"I don't know what happened. I was standing on the stage and suddenly I went flying through the air. That's the last time I turn my back on the band.

"Actually it was heat prostration. I black out every time I stand close to Carroll Baker.

"No, it wasn't really a fall. When I bow, I *bow!*

"There've been a lot of wild rumors that we may have to cancel our trip to Vietnam. I oughta know . . . I started them!

"This is quite a distinction. How many guys go to Vietnam to *heal?*

"But all the gals have been wonderful to me since I hurt my ankle. As Shakespeare said, 'Sweet are the uses of adversity.' You all remember Shakespeare—one of Jack Benny's early writers.

"Incidentally, I wanna thank the GI who caught me and

84

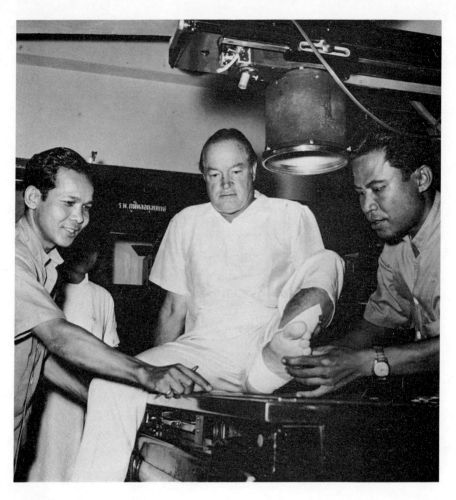

*Two of the Cong fitting me for a broken ankle. (NBC Photo by Gary Null)*

broke my fall. I'm gonna do that as soon as he gets out of the guardhouse."

That night, the entire troupe was invited to an evening cruise aboard a ship of the Royal Thai Navy. Our host was my golfing companion, Air Marshal Dawee. Dinner and drinks were served as we sailed along the Klong River toward the Gulf of Siam. It was a cool, relaxing evening and everything went beautifully until we returned to Bangkok and prepared to dock. For some reason, they couldn't maneuver the boat into its berth. After three or four unsuccessful attempts, a few of our people began to shout instructions to the crew telling them the right way to dock the boat. This may sound presumptuous, but you must remember that these backseat navigators were seasoned mariners. Some of them had even sailed to Catalina on "the big white steamship," and one or two had braved the treacherous waters of New York Harbor aboard the Staten Island ferry, so this gratuitous advice was backed by years of inexperience.

Finally, the helmsman, with Mort Lachman at his side mumbling advice through his pipe, was able to nose the boat into its slip, to loud cheers and applause. It was no accident that Mort's help did the trick. Known as the Aristotle Onassis of Sherman Oaks, Mort once wrote some material for the Yacht Club Boys.

# CHAPTER FOUR

Friday, December 24, was the day before Christmas. Check your calendars. I'm sure I'm right about this. It was also a big day for goose pimples. Our destination was top secret, but everybody had a pretty good hunch we weren't on the way to Geneva for a peace conference. I know I lit two candles the night before and it wasn't to read by.

Our big C-141 was headed for Vietnam, and nobody in the cast or crew seemed anxious to climb on board. I don't know whether it's true that a coward dies a thousand deaths, but I'll tell you one thing, we had a lot of wounded loitering in the shade of the plane wings.

We were headed for combat and just to get in the mood, we had a little hand-to-hand battle right on the runway. We had allowed an extra half hour just for loading the Bangkok loot, and it was barely enough time. Our cast and crew are all experienced travelers . . . it's amazing how they get carried away and buy all kinds of ridiculous things when they go to a foreign country. I know, I've seen it all before and I only buy things that I really need. All I picked up this trip to Bangkok was a hammered brass bath mat, a teakwood throne, a silver elephant whistle, a twelve-foot cobra skin, a mother-of-pearl brandy snifter, and a rattan bread box.

The rest of the cast and crew were ridiculous.

Finally, just before takeoff, the loadmaster came over to Sil Caranchini, our advance man and inventor of stomach acid, and informed him that if there were any more packages brought on, the plane just could not get off the ground.

Our pilot was very concerned. His license didn't cover flying a department store.

We were given the signal to board and we all got on the plane. All except, of course, the one who is perpetually late and missing. . . . That's right . . . the last of the Irish Mau Mau, Barney McNulty. When Barney was born, instead of a baby there was a note saying, "Have gone to the PX. Be back in two hours."

Sil stood at the door checking his watch and staring angrily, waiting for Barney to appear. Finally a truck came roaring up and out came Barney. He staggered up the ramp with a huge package in his arms, and Sil had really had it. He stood in the doorway, barring Barney's entrance to the plane, and said, "Barney, I've warned you for the last time. You've got parcels all over this plane. You buy ten times what everybody else in the troupe buys. The plane's overloaded. We can't carry another ounce. You're not getting on the plane with that package. What's in it?"

Barney was quite calm about the whole thing, looked Sil squarely in the face, and said, "In this package I have marking pens, black ink, and idiot cards with which I do the monologue cards for Bob." Sil stared at him, Barney stared back, Sil stepped out of the way, Barney stepped into the plane with his package, and we took off for Saigon.

As the crow flies, it's only four hundred miles from Bangkok to Saigon. Of course, the crow loses a few tail feathers over neutral Laos and Cambodia. We could also have saved a little time by using the Ho Chi Minh Trail. But you know how I hate those crowded freeways. We took the long way around . . . out over the Gulf of Siam. A half hour out of Saigon's Tan Son Nhut Airport, we received word from the cockpit that we had a fighter escort. I don't know if we were getting the red carpet treatment or whether they were essential, but we sure gave those crazy jets a big cheer.

*A selection from my live bait tank. (NBC Photo by Frank Carroll)*

When you arrive at a commercial airport on a regular flight, you drop down at a nice smooth one thousand feet a minute. In Vietnam they don't dig those long, slow descents. You're too much of a target at the end of a runway. So our crew was ordered to drop our C-141 from six thousand feet to the runway in less than a minute. The teen-agers have a term for this. It's called "group sky diving" or "suicide can be fun." It was the first time it had ever been tried with a C-141, and I have to give the crew credit. Both the plane and my stomach hit the runway at the same time.

Normally when we arrive at a base, Clay Daniel, our

laconic, sour-faced assistant director from the Deep South, gets up and announces, "The camera crew will get off first, and then the cast, led by Mistuh Hope." I insist on this as a matter of protocol, so I can introduce the rest of the cast to any civil or military dignitaries who happen to be there to welcome us. The truth of the matter is, I get off first so that somebody knows I'm there. Once they see the girls, I might as well be a leper.

When we landed at Tan Son Nhut, our first combat base, Clay stood up and said, "We will deplane in the following order: First the cameramen, then the technical crew, then the production staff, then the band, then the cast, then the women, then the children, then Mr. Bob Hope." He got a pretty big laugh, which is nice for a fellow making his last trip.

Tan Son Nhut has got to be one of the busiest airports in the world. It swings twenty-four hours a day. On one side of the field is the civilian terminal where all the commercial liners come in. The other side of the field is the military air base, both Vietnamese and American. On the field you see every kind of airplane in the world, and a few that haven't been invented yet. Commercial liners, propjets, jet bombers, jet fighters, 'copters of every kind and description. It looks like Eddie Rickenbacker's rumpus room.

The control tower answers the pilots in three languages . . . Vietnamese, French, and English. If they answer in Chinese, you look for another airport.

The entire perimeter of the field is surrounded by barbed wire. It is further protected by mines, watchtowers, and sandbagged machine gun nests. It is patrolled around the clock. And small wonder, for it is an inviting target for the Cong. Even on the dullest of days they lob in a few mortar shells just to keep their chipping sharp. The main gate has been blown up three times—but you know the military. Nobody gets in without a pass. And yet, strangely, you have the feeling that this is the safest place you can be in Vietnam.

There are several thousand civilian employees on the base, and since the Cong look like anybody else in Vietnam, you could see this would pose quite a security problem. The Vietnamese Air Force has an ingenious answer. They use the same solution as the Hollywood film studios use for keeping out the enemy . . . they only hire relatives.

They really had the welcome mat out for us. As I stepped off the plane, I was greeted by General Ben Sternberg, Aide to General Westmoreland, and by his staff. This was a real tribute, since the General had seen our show last year. There were escort officers and project officers, all wearing "Big Cheer" tags on their uniforms. This was the secret code name assigned to our troupe during its stay in Vietnam. I hoped the code name would prove to be an apt description of the show. The secret code name assigned to me was "The Man." I also hoped that this would prove to be an apt description of me while I was in Vietnam.

Also crowded around the plane were hundreds of GIs, mechanics and technicians, lots of photographers and press, and also two very familiar faces. One was Johnny Grant, my very good caloric friend from KMPC in Los Angeles, who has taken out so many U.S.O. tours to troops around the world. At this time Johnny was over in Vietnam taping interviews with the GIs. And there was Martha Raye. Pardon me, I mean "Colonel" Martha Raye. Martha had already been over three weeks, thumbing airlifts from remote base to remote base. Not a big show . . . just Martha and two GI musicians. What am I talking about, "not a big show"? When you've got Martha you don't need anything else.

As first I didn't recognize Martha. She was wearing combat boots, an old fatigue outfit, and an old fatigue hat to protect her from the sun, and to protect the sun against Martha. She had her silver oak leaves on her shoulder, so

*I play flower girl for Martha and Johnny Grant. (NBC Photo by Gary Null)*

the newspaper stories were true . . . Martha was really a Colonel . . . God help the Cong!

At first I thought that Martha was wounded, then I realized she had her mouth open. She couldn't believe the reception our show troupe had gotten at the airport. "You should have seen what happened when *I* arrived," said Martha. "We got here about two o'clock in the morning, I staggered off the plane with my suitcase . . . last . . . and by the time I got down to the runway there wasn't a soul around. I didn't know which way to go. I sat on my suitcase and waited for somebody to show up. Finally, about a half hour later, a lone GI in a Jeep pulled up next to the plane. 'You Martha Raye?' he said. I said, 'Yeah, I'm Martha Raye. I'm glad to see you. Who are you?' He just stared at me and said, 'Throw your suitcase in the back of the Jeep and let's go. I'm late.' He dumped me off at an airport terminal and I had to wait until eight o'clock in the morning for someone to show up."

Of course, that's all changed now. Martha is the toast of Vietnam. The favorite housemother of GIs everywhere. I think she'd be there yet if she hadn't run out of silver polish for her oak leaves.

During the shows I did a joke about the wonderful protection we were getting from the Military Police. How they had twenty-five men with machine guns guarding the girls and for the fellows they had a midget with a slingshot. From the time we stepped off that plane in Saigon, we really *did* have security. There was an escort assigned to every member of the cast and that escort officer was armed. Whenever we moved *anywhere* in Vietnam, we moved in convoy. And in addition to armed drivers in every car, there were military police in Jeeps ahead of us and behind us and around us.

If we weren't nervous when we got off the plane, we certainly were when we saw all the security precautions that were taken just to get us to a press conference on the base. There we had the whole cast on a small stage, and we answered questions from the American press, American television, and the Vietnamese press. I'll be honest with you, I don't remember a word that anybody said. Every time that one of those photographers popped a flashbulb I went into orbit. Usually when it comes to photographers I'm a pretty good strategist, and I usually wind up with my kisser in the center of the lens. This was one time I kept the girls up front and said "cheese" from the background. I was really happy for my vaudeville training. I could dodge and

*We had twenty MPs for the girls . . . and a midget with a slingshot for me. (NBC Photo by Frank Carroll)*

make it look like I was dancing . . . although many critics say it's the other way around.

After the press conference we were joined at lunch by one of the great Americans of our generation . . . the Commander of all U.S. forces in Vietnam, General William Childs Westmoreland. Here's a guy who's got it all . . . personality, brains, and muscle when he needs it. He respects his men, and, more important, they respect him. A lot of us had had the pleasure of meeting the General the year before, and he gave us a great welcome.

As we reached the end of lunch, I started to get my "show twitch." I knew we were going to have one of our biggest crowds at Tan Son Nhut, and I was anxious to get started. Just then our balloon-bellied advance man and coordinator John Pawlek walked into the dining room. I started to get up to hustle the show to the show site. John stopped me. "We got about another half hour to go, Bob, so take your time."

"Another half hour!" I screamed, but smiling at the same time so he'd still know it was lovable me. "Why aren't we set up? Why aren't we ready to go?"

John said, "We only have one plane. It takes the technical crew an hour and a half to set up, and they got here on the same plane with the cast."

"But I've just been talking to the General here, and he says we can have anything we want . . . if we want two planes from Bangkok to Saigon we can have them. They're ours. All you have to do is ask for them, John."

And John said, "Your friend the General says we can have them, but my friend, the Sergeant, says we can't."

Everybody broke up, including the General, who pounded the table. It's my own fault. That's what I get for hiring a noncommissioned audio engineer.

The first year we played Tan Son Nhut we did our show right on the runway. And I did my monologue practically in the landing pattern. This year we were in the soccer

*General Westmoreland, his staff, and five cadets from the Pink Pussy-cat East. (NBC Photo by Gary Null)*

field, and the stage was built on the bed of a military truck-trailer. The crowd was estimated anywhere from five to twelve thousand. All I know was as far as you could see there were Air Force, Marines, Army, hospital patients in blue pajamas, there were Aussies in their "Go-to-Hell" hats, Embassy civilians, Vietnamese dignitaries, green berets, nurses, doctors . . . a sea of people broiling in the sun. I looked at the band on stage. They were a very unhealthy shade of purple. And they were going to get another good two and a half hours of baking. And then I realized the tune they were playing . . . "I've Got My Love to Keep Me Warm."

Brigadier General George B. Sempler opened the show in Vietnamese fashion: "*Choi-oi,* everybody, and a big *choi-oi,* Air Marshal Ky, General Westmoreland, ladies and gentlemen. On behalf of the Armed Forces and the Republic of Vietnam, the United States and the free world, it is my pleasure to introduce you to Bing Crosby's Commanding Officer . . . Bob 'the original red-nosed reindeer' Hope." The audience was most generous with their applause, and as I stood there and took my bow, I looked out in the audience and sure enough, there were at least five signs saying, "Welcome Bing Crosby." I don't care where I play . . . from the biggest base in the United States to the most remote outpost in the jungle, it's always there . . . the sign that says, "Welcome Bing Crosby."

I held up my hands and said, "Please, not too much applause. I'd hate to be held over. Here I am, the longest delivery Chicken Delight ever made. This is my second time in Saigon, which puts me in the same class with our Ambassador. He's also a twotime loser. I'm happy to be here. I understand everything's great. The situation's improved . . . in fact, things couldn't be better." Then I had to pause for the hissing and booing, and then I finished with, "Who am I gonna believe . . . you or Huntley and Brinkley?"

Like GIs everywhere, these guys really dug the jokes that were about them, about Vietnam, about Saigon, about the bases where they were stationed, the service they were in . . . anything about the military. But these guys were also very hip and bright about everything that's happening around the world. It's only a one-year tour of duty, and many of them had just come over from the States, many of them would soon be returning there. And they were extremely interested in everything about home . . . especially the student demonstrations, draft card burnings, and the Vietniks. There was a tremendous response to lines like:

"The student demonstrations have calmed down. They ran out of matches.

"The Government's got a new policy about burning draft cards. They now say, 'If he's old enough to play with matches, draft him.'

"We've had all kinds of demonstrations back in the States . . . 'Get out of Vietnam,' 'Don't get out of Vietnam,' 'Why don't you go back where you came from?' and 'I came from Vietnam, that's why.'

"Those kids protest against anything. I saw a kid carrying a picket sign that said, 'Girls are unfair.' I marched twenty-five miles with him.

"Actually, I was very lucky. I went to my North Hollywood draft board, and they gave me a thorough physical. I thought they were pretty rude about it. They burned my draft card."

At the finish I would explain that only a small percentage were involved in the demonstrations and that the vast majority of the people at home were not only proud but grateful for the wonderful job they were doing.

If there's one thing I really get a kick out of it's free loot. It's not that I'm penurious, I would be, but that's Jack Benny's bit. I guess everybody secretly believes in Santa Claus, and I've really been lucky. For me it's Christmas practically every day of the year. I've received literally tons of gifts . . . medallions, scrolls, plaques, statues, portraits, even a goatskin rug. Last year at Nha Trang they presented me with a Viet Cong machine gun. I don't know whether it was a gift or a hint. And I'm really a hoarder. I enjoy it all and keep it all on display in my office in North Hollywood. The floor sank a foot last year. The room looks like Tiffany's backfired. As Dolores has said to me many times, "If only you were a failure we could save a fortune in dust cloths."

However, there are certain times when the awards can be a little embarrassing. And the Christmas shows are one of them. When I'm standing out there on that stage I'm surrounded by a great cast and a fantastic crew that numbers over sixty. They've all given up their Christmas at home to travel to a combat zone. The quarters aren't much, the weather's usually miserable, the hours are endless, yet they work their fannies off for the show. And they're all volunteers. None of them had to go. They come because they want to. Take the guys in the band. They don't make a helluva lot of dough during the year, and Christmas and New Year at home are when they get most of their bookings. They could make three times the bread by staying at home and never being more than a mile from the "Whiskey-A-Go-Go." But they're hooked like all these other gypsies on the box lunches. And these great gals who could get this same guest star pay doing one show in Burbank, come out to these hot jungles to work to a hotter audience, because they feel it's the thing to do.

I guess that's one of the reasons why I'm such an ardent fan of General Westmoreland. He gets up at six o'clock every morning and works through till midnight . . . and that's seven days a week. He's got more problems than an astronaut with acrophobia. And yet, at the end of the show at Tan Son Nhut he came up on stage and thanked every member of the cast by name. He thanked the band, and he thanked the crew. He shook hands with every member of the cast and handed them a plaque with their name inscribed. And then the riot started . . . Carroll Baker threw her arms around the General and kissed him on the lips. The crowd roared. And then it was follow the leader . . . Kaye planted one on him, Anita planted one on him . . . Joey bussed him, even Diana gave him a kiss on the cheek. The audience was on its feet, stamping, whistling, yelling, and applauding.

Just as things started to simmer down, the General shook

*"Don't shoot—he's on our side!"* (*NBC Photo by Gary Null*)

hands with and presented a plaque to Jerry Colonna. "The Brush" leaned over and planted a kiss on the General's ear. And that was it . . . absolute bedlam. Fortunately, the cameras were rolling and we were able to use this segment on our television show. I hope you saw it. In the midst of a tough and ugly and dangerous situation, here was a warm, wonderful, flippy moment. When Anita led us in "Silent Night," there were lots of tears, but at least this time some of them were from laughter.

Backstage, after the show, General Westmoreland introduced me to Premier Nguyen Cao Ky and his wife. Since the fall of President Diem in 1963, there have been nineteen government reshuffles in Saigon. In fact, I had a line, "Vietnam is one of the real democracies . . . everybody gets to be President." Fortunately, I didn't do it with Premier Ky in the audience. But he's had his troubles. He's been in more hot water than a bachelor in Tokyo.

People have asked me what I thought of this controversial figure. Frankly, there isn't much I can say. It was a very short meeting. He is an extremely handsome man . . . a cross between Frankie Avalon and David Niven. I understand he's a favorite pinup of the Vietnam WACs, and that when he goes out on the street he gets screams from the teen-agers. He also gets screams from the Buddhists, but that's another story. It's an all Air Force family. He was one of Vietnam's hot jet jockeys, and his beautiful young wife is a former Air Vietnam stewardess. I used to do a story about the non-sched airline that couldn't afford to show movies . . . they just left the door open so you could watch the pilot and the stewardess. I guess it's the same the world over.

The Premier was most cordial. He presented me with a vase usually awarded to an outstanding squadron in his Air Force. It's the first time I've been honored for bombing.

When Mary Martin appeared in Vietnam, Premier Ky presented her with a huge teakwood and lacquer plaque with an historical story and scene of the country on the topside. It was about the size of a coffee table, and weighed a ton. Men are men whether it's in Shubert Alley or a jungle in Vietnam. At my show he was a distinguished visitor. But when Mary Martin showed up he was just another stage-door Nguyen.

Imagine taking a show like *Hello, Dolly!* into the jungles of Vietnam! I've heard of "Off Broadway," but this is ridiculous! It was a great achievement of the Defense Department to put that show on complete in every detail. Our show is considered heavy, but we were just a Gus Sun

*General Westmoreland, me, Marshal Ky, the charming Madame Ky, and a trophy from my favorite "Ky" club. (NBC Photo by Gary Null)*

repertoire company compared to their elaborate staging. They had it all . . . big beautiful sets, old-fashioned costumes, and a tremendous cast, including singers and dancers. The first time the chorus girls came on stage, fourteen snipers fell out of the trees.

After our show I posed for a picture with the Premier and General Westmoreland. The photo is now on display at neighborhood post offices all over North Vietnam, with a reward listed below. I understand the Cong will pay two hundred dollars for an American GI's head, five hundred for a field officer, a thousand for a General, and for an actor they'll swap you a little monkey meat—even.

Vietnam, of course, is now the number one resort of the government VIP tour. There have been so many VIPs in Saigon that General Westmoreland has to sleep in his dress blues. If you didn't know better, you'd think that General Hershey was drafting Congressmen.

Senator Fulbright came to Vietnam and got his own television series. It's a quiz show with Secretary McNamara as the mystery guest. Senator Fulbright said that Saigon has become an American brothel, and that many Vietnamese have been forced, through GI-caused inflation, to put up their wives and daughters as bar girls and mistresses. That's the story of my life. After I get *back* from Saigon, Senator Fulbright tells me where the action is. I get the feeling I'm in the wrong branch of the entertainment business.

During the Senate investigations on television, Senator Fulbright asked Secretary McNamara how it was that one PX in Vietnam alone had ordered ten thousand cans of hair spray. Secretary McNamara explained that it was an error in judgment on the part of the PX manager, and that he was "no longer in our employ." Many of the military believe otherwise. They regard cans of hair spray as a vital strategic material which may go a long way in determining the eventual course of the war. Just as the Hershey bar and nylon stockings played their part in former wars, a push-button can of hair spray is far superior to the carbine when it comes to hand-to-hand in-fighting. As one GI explained to me, "This battle will not be won by bullets alone. It is our job to win these people over to democracy. And I am concentrating on the women." He was short, fat, ugly, and bald. And he looked blissfully happy. He must know whereof he speaks.

One of the reasons I went to Vietnam was to see my Congressman. But he was back home in Los Angeles study-

*"If she gets any of that on me, I'll scream."* (NBC Photo by Gary Null)

ing drama and taking tap-dancing lessons. However, I did have the pleasure of meeting Representative Thomas C. McGrath, Jr., the Congressman from the 2nd District in New Jersey. We also posed for some pictures together, along with our former bathing beauty contest winner, Anita Bryant. The Congressman presented me with a plaque and pair of bathing trunks and made me an official honorary lifeguard at Atlantic City. So if you're ever in Vietnam and need an Atlantic City lifeguard, let me know. It's the only place I'm licensed to practice. Please make a reservation before drowning. They only gave me the one pair of trunks.

By the time I'd finished my diplomatic chores backstage and Pete and Jerry and Jack had finished signing autographs, the girls were dressed and ready to move on. We got in our Jeep convoy and headed for the Third Field Hospital. When you read the casualty statistics in the paper they're just that . . . statistics. But when you see them in person, you're shocked right to the bone marrow.

It's true, our medical corps is doing a fantastic job, thanks to the helicopter. Twenty minutes after a man is wounded he is in the hospital. With the new flying cranes they can now take an operating room, complete with surgeons and nurses, and drop it right in the battle area. And then *lift* the mobile operating room and return it to the hospital. With this new air-evacuating procedure, with the new surgical techniques, and the new drugs, the recovery percentage is miraculous. But, unfortunately, the miracles don't include growing a new leg to replace the one that's been blown off, or to provide a new optic nerve for one that's been severed by a mortar shell.

The first kid I talked to had been ripped in the stomach by a pungi stick. That's a cute little Cong weapon . . . a bamboo stake that's been sharpened to a point and dipped in human excrement. Primitive, but deadly effective. After the kid had been wounded, he had been covered with sand and left to die. He wasn't in great shape when they carried him in, but he was going to make it. The next patient was a 'copter pilot. He got it from ground fire . . . in the leg. He was thrilled about it. He pointed to his leg and said, "Look, Bob, there's my Christmas present. A trip home."

That's the great thing about these kids . . . they've still got their sense of humor. When they talk to you, they don't want sympathy, they want to exchange some laughs, and if they can top you, they really get a kick out of it. So when you're walking through the wards, you just keep it cool and flip on the outside, no matter how you feel on the inside. And you just keep thanking your God that you're not on the wrong side of those hospital sheets.

For some of our gals, it was their first hospital tour. On the way over in the convoy they were very quiet and obviously nervous. But you should have seen them when they walked into those wards. . . . They really took over. In one ward there were fourteen guys that all got it at the same time. They'd been riding down the highway when an eleven-year-old Vietnamese kid tossed a grenade into their truck. Most of them were badly torn up. Two had lost their legs. According to GI scuttlebutt, the kid who threw the grenade got fifty cents from the Cong. In America he'd be pitching for the Little League.

In one bed was a GI, actually a kid of about twenty-one who had severe internal injuries. He was about ten minutes away from the operating room, and he was plenty scared. Carroll Baker walked over to his bed and he grabbed her hand and he didn't release her until the pills took over and put him out. That's my kind of kid. He knew what to latch on to even when he was under an anesthetic.

As we walked from bed to bed, the doctor would point out the different kids . . . when they'd arrived and what their trouble was. We stopped in front of one bed and the doctor said, "This boy hasn't smiled since he's been here." I shook his hand, laid a few jokes on him, and he just kind of grunted and turned away. I couldn't get to him. Then up bounced Kaye Stevens, yelling, "Hiya!—Wee wee wow wow!" Real wide-open Western style. She looked down at this kid, grabbed him, and gave him a great big kiss. "How do you feel now?" she asked. And the kid looked up with a smile as big as Kaye's and said, "I feel pretty good right now!" The doctor said to me, "I don't believe it." I did. Never underestimate the power of a woman. But not even Kaye could win them all. Here's her story about "Frenchy":

106

"I'd race down the aisles between the beds, and to each boy I'd say, 'Hey, you got a kiss for Christmas?' And they'd say, 'Yeah.' And I'd give them a kiss and say, 'Are you trying to put me on? You're not sick.' This one boy, Frenchy, was a real sick kid. One arm was gone and an ear had been blasted off. I went up to him and I said, 'Merry Christmas.' And he scowled at me and said, 'What's there to be merry about? What's so merry about Merry Christmas?' And I said, 'You're alive, aren't you, stupid? Merry Christmas!' And he just looked at me and I looked at him, and we reached an impasse. Then I walked away and I kept looking back at him and he kept looking at me, but he didn't say anything, and I didn't give him his Christmas kiss. I got a smile out of every kid in that ward, but I couldn't get to Frenchy. When I walked out of the ward he was staring at me. And I couldn't get it out of my mind. That sad face . . . those huge eyes, just staring."

# CHAPTER FIVE

Some of the world's immortal literature has been written on the walls of latrines. My new favorite is this one which I found scrawled in the washroom of an enlisted men's billet: "Forever Is A Day In Saigon."

In the face of life's normal trials and tribulations I am as stanch and resolute as a bowl of gelatine. But when it comes to real danger, I go right to St. Vitus. In Saigon I shake *all* the time. I peer nervously out of windows. . . . I listen for footsteps in the hall. If a car backfires or there's a sudden knock on the door, I run down to the lobby and surrender to the bell captain.

Out in the street you walk as if you're on eggs. You look nervously ahead and behind you. You're jumpy about the sound of your own footsteps echoing on the pavement. You never know when some guy's gonna recognize you and hate you from another war.

The whole city's like that. Everybody walks close to the buildings along the sidewalks because it's easier to find shelter in a doorway. After curfew everybody moves fast. The whole city is one big Olympics.

Anybody can be a Cong terrorist . . . an old man, a pretty gal . . . a little kid with a paper sack. The enemy is always close. Of course, I should be used to that. In my act, they usually are. It's an impossible city for a coward. Can you imagine me not knowing which way to run?

You can't tell the Cong from any friendly Vietnamese. You just take your chance. It's the Oriental version of Russian roulette. And they're not the least bit fussy about who they blow up. They have the same problem we do, only in reverse. To the Cong, all "round eyes" look alike.

They call Saigon "The Paris of the East." There are a lot of sidewalk cafes. Of course, they didn't start out on the sidewalk. It's the original boom-boom city. They really have the answer to urban renewal—TNT. It's the only place in the world where a woman can get dressed in thirty seconds flat. But it's a miserable city for a postman . . . it's not easy sorting in midair. Instead of the people changing their address, the buildings do! It's a real resort city. A great place to come for a rest . . . especially if you want a long one.

Saigon is one of the oldest cities in the world, and they've got the plumbing to prove it. Once a beautiful and charming French colonial town of four hundred thousand, it is now a hot, steaming mess of two million people, its population swollen with thousands of refugees and the military. It has one of the densest populations in the world, and you really know it if you ever walk into a crowded elevator or room and are assaulted by the aroma of "nook-mom."

The Vietnamese use nook-mom the way we use catsup. It is their national favorite. A delicious sauce made out of fish heads and lighter fluid. The smell is unbelievably potent. You eat it with a fork and a clothes pin. It chews the meat before you can. It's got a range of about sixty yards. Unfortunately, the Geneva Convention won't let them breathe on the enemy.

Saigon has been playing host to foreign armies for the last twenty-five years. All they have to do is change the signs in front of the bars. There are over five thousand bars in Saigon right now. I know . . . the Les Brown Band counted them. And they all have American names like "The San Francisco Bar," "The Seattle Bar," "The Yankee Bar." In fact, you can see the effect of the Americans almost everywhere. One of the most popular restaurants is called

"Cheap Charley's." There's also a Howard Johnson Restaurant . . . "Sears Tailors" . . . "Hart Schaffner Tailors" and "The Texas Laundry." None are in any way connected with their U.S. namesakes. But they all have one common purpose . . . to shear the GI lamb.

The traffic is absurd. The five o'clock rush hour is twenty-four hours a day. You can ride for fifty miles through the narrow, congested, honking streets without leaving the scene of the accident. One-way streets? Forget it. It's every man for himself.

The sides of an automobile never get dirty. The city is so overcrowded that as you drive down the narrow streets you actually brush against people's clothing. The people are so used to it that they don't even notice you or your car. It's like going through the brushes in a car wash. If you don't have a tire mark on your foot, you're a tourist.

Big cars, little cars, trucks, motor scooters, cycles, pedicabs, buses . . . all tangled in a helpless, honking snarl. And through it all you see the exquisite Vietnamese women in pastel silks pedaling serenely by on their bicycles.

About those gals . . . believe me, Vietnam is solid Louisa May Alcott country . . . all little women, all beautiful. They seem to have found some kind of secret. They all look the same whether they're fifteen or fifty . . . not a wrinkle, all beautiful, all trim and slim-figured. We found out why all the men there have slant eyes. It's those slit skirts the women wear.

In case you managed to survive the bombings, the B-girls, and the traffic, you're perfectly safe for as long as you want to stay in Saigon . . . just as long as you don't eat or drink. Do you think I'm kidding? Get a load of this happy little notice that's handed out by our military:

"In all areas of Vietnam, including Saigon, water is not fit for drinking. This includes water used in restaurants, as well as tap water in hotels. Ice is also contaminated and should be avoided. Milk products should be avoided because most of the cattle are diseased. Beer and wine are okay as long as you don't drink out of a glass. Those are also contaminated." Of course, this was no problem to the band; they're all bottle babies.

When it comes to the food in restaurants you're not a lot better off, according to the military. They suggest you avoid leafy vegetables. They harbor amoebic cysts. Do not eat any salad dressings; no raw fruits or vegetables. Most of the meat in Vietnam is contaminated with worms. Of course, all of this was no hardship for me. I find that in times of stress and strain my fingernails contain the minimum daily requirements suggested by the United States Food and Drug Administration.

I don't think I'll ever forget our first visit to Saigon. That was in Christmas of '64. We certainly opened with a bang, although we didn't know it at the time. Our convoy had a military escort into Saigon. There was an armed Jeep ahead of us, and two behind us, with MPs manning machine guns. The sirens were wailing, red lights flashing, they had all the stops out, and we were flying through the Saigon traffic at at least two or three miles an hour. Sometimes we'd go almost a block before we were caught in another jam.

It was like threading a needle with a garden hose . . . or sucking a walnut through a straw. We were trying like hell, but we weren't getting very far. I was riding in the lead car with Major General Joe Moore, who's the head of the Air Force over there and now a lieutenant general, his wife, and Jerry Colonna.

About five minutes from the hotel our convoy came to a complete halt. And there seemed to be a big commotion. The General called the MP back from the Jeep in front of us and asked what was going on. The MP answered that according to what he heard on his walkie-talkie, there was a fire.

We were stopped there for about ten minutes and were

*When I work nobody walks out. (NBC Photo by Frank Carroll)*

told to close all the car windows. Inasmuch as it was about 105 degrees inside the car, I suggested as long as we were stopped it might be good to let in a little fresh air. General Joe agreed with my thinking but reminded me that at the moment we made a very conspicuous target and that the Cong would like nothing better than to drop a little pineapple into the car. My window flew closed by itself, and I sat there enjoying the heat. Those are the wonderful little moments that keep you on your toes.

Suddenly there was a loud bang and the windshield cracked. We all hit the floor. Then, when there was no explosion, we looked out and spotted a five-year-old, half-naked kid running away. He had thrown a rock at our car. I don't know if the others were scared, but I turned on General Moore and yelled, "Go home, Yank!"

When we pulled up at the Caravelle Hotel there were huge crowds milling in front. There was a cordon of police, the Vietnamese "White Mice," there were MPs and guards, barbed wire, sandbags in front of the building. Naturally a modest man, I was amazed at the size of my reception, and all the trouble that people had gone to. I waved gaily to the crowd, taking a few walking bows, and was pushed rather abruptly into the hotel and escorted directly to my room.

Now that I think back about it, I realize that the windows in the lobby were smashed, there was debris all over, and there was considerable hysteria. However, at the time either these details didn't register, or I just put it down to the Caravelle being a great party hotel.

When I got up to the room, my traveling therapist, Freddy Miron, the Dr. Schweitzer of the sacroiliac, was all excited. He was trying to tell me something about a bombing. It wasn't too clear to me. Freddy is a native enchiladan, and when he gets nervous his meaning loses a little something in the translation. I said, "Don't try to dramatize things, Fred; what do you mean, 'a bomb'? It was a fire. You heard the MP. He said it was a fire."

Freddy said, "I don't care whether you're Bob Hope or not, it was a bombing!" I don't know why he keeps getting so personal. I said, "Freddy, you keep building things up, you're always trying to make hysterical things out of nothing. It was a little fire down the street, they got a little ambulance, they got a little smoke, and that's all there is to it. Just relax and go swat some lizards!"

Then there was a rap at the door and in walked three very serious-looking guys from the demolition squad. They were a little close-mouthed about the details, but they announced that there had been a bombing. They really searched that room. I didn't mind them checking my luggage, but they asked me to say "Ah." Before that trip was over I was frisked so many times I was starting to like it.

Freddy and I were warned not to accept any gifts from strangers, not to allow anyone to pack our luggage, not to allow anyone else to carry it, to stay away from windows, keep the drapes closed, and in case of an explosion to hit the floor. I was also told to wear my dog tags at all times. I didn't have any dog tags, but I did wear my combination St. Christopher's medal and mezuzah. I'm a guy who takes all the odds.

The bombing occurred at Brink's Hotel, about a block from us in downtown Saigon. It housed some 125 people, including American officers. A Cong terrorist had about three hundred pounds of TNT which he put into a Jeep and rolled into a garage under the hotel. The blast had occurred about twenty minutes before our arrival at our hotel, and shattered and cracked windows and buildings in an area about half a mile square. Wreckage from several vehicles was found scattered a block and a half away. Mangled pieces of metal were left hanging on power lines about the area. We didn't know it then, but some 107 people were injured, including Americans and Vietnamese.

I did a little thinking. I was on the hook for quite a group of people, and I hoped I hadn't gotten their fat in the fire. I had no way of knowing whether this was a one-shot, or if the Cong was doing a series. I pulled the drapes in the room first, and then peeked out the window. I was right on the corner overlooking the bombing. There were three trees growing right up alongside my window. I was on the fourth floor. They had already bombed the fifth floor of the hotel previously. I closed the drapes.

I opened my door and peeked out. There was a Vietnamese guard standing there with a submachine gun pointed at almost anybody. I wasn't sure whether he was put there to protect me or Jill St. John. I smiled at him, but he wouldn't smile back. I wasn't sure whether he was on our side or not. Every time I'd walk out to the elevator I'd look at him and try to give him my opening vaudeville smile that I used at the Earl Theatre . . . and died with. He'd just stare right back at me. For the three days we were there, we had our own private cold war.

The rest of the cast was having its problems, too. Anita Bryant was just taking a shower when the security men started through her room, looked under the bed, in the light fixtures, in the closet, and finally in the bathroom, where they found Anita dripping wet and holding up a towel to cover her. One of them was really ecstatic. He said, "Hey, you're Anita Bryant, aren't you? I'm from Oklahoma, too. And I know your cousin Alfred. We went to school together. What's old Alfy doing?"

He put out his hand to shake hands with her, and Anita started to but remembered just in time to hang on to the towel. But since these were bosom buddies of good old cousin Alfred, Anita was most cordial. She sent the guys happily along the way, each with an autographed copy of her latest album. It wasn't until after the door closed behind them that Anita realized she didn't have a cousin Alfred.

*That'll teach Jill St. John to play poker with the band. (NBC Photo by Frank Carroll)*

Jerry Colonna had heard all the warnings we had. He went to his room and found the door unlocked. He didn't know whether to enter or not. But he'd seen "The Man from U.N.C.L.E." He opened the door and stepped away. There were no shots. He entered the room, and he was conscious there had been someone there. And then he spotted it . . . a strange package sitting on the desk. He wanted to call for help, but he was afraid the telephone might be booby-trapped. He did the only sensible thing. He screamed.

If you've ever heard the Colonna scream, and, judging by our ratings, you have, you know that one note from him can break glass throughout the building. MPs, guards, and demolition men crowded into his room. They congratulated Colonna on his sagacity in calling them, and while most of them hid behind mattresses, one brave lieutenant grabbed the package, took it into the bathroom, and dumped it into a tub of water. The explosion was minor when they opened the package. It was a plaque from General Westmoreland which had been delivered to Colonna's room. You can see the plaque today in Jerry's apartment on Sunset Boulevard. It's there, but it's a little warped.

The band was not so lucky. They stayed at the Continental Palace, just a few doors down from the devastated Brink's Hotel. They had no electricity at all, and no water. The glass from the windows had all been blown out and onto the rugs and the beds. Before they could go to bed they had to turn their beds over to get the glass out. They slept in their clothes.

I asked Butch Stone, our beloved "band mother," if we shouldn't do something . . . if we shouldn't get the band out of this terrible disaster area. He said, "Are you kidding, Bob? You couldn't get the boys out of there. It reminds them of home."

Meanwhile, down in the shattered lobby, the high command was holding a super-secret strategy meeting. General

Ben Sternberg and his staff were conferring with Colonels Larry Glaab and "Red" Beasley, our Project Officers, as to whether they should cancel the shows and keep us underground for a couple of days, or sneak us on a plane and get us the hell back to Thailand.

Colonel Glaab said, "Well, they couldn't possibly put on shows here. The young ladies in the troupe must be in a terrible state of shock."

At this point, Jill St. John and Janis Paige walked up and appeared to be in a very agitated state. Jill turned to General Sternberg and said, "Sergeant, it's a terrible emergency. My camera's locked in the plane, and I want to take pictures of the bombing."

And Janis said, "And while you're out there, will you get my red dancing pumps? I'll need them tomorrow at Vinh Long, or whatever secret base we're going to play. (Of course, it happened to be Vinh Long.)

The General and the Colonel adjourned to the corner to re-evaluate the situation. On the basis of what they had just seen, the shows would go on as scheduled. The brass had no need to worry. If they had tried to stop those girls, they would have had another war on their hands.

That evening we were all scheduled to go to Ambassador Maxwell Taylor's. But because of the tenseness of the situation that was canceled, as well as our annual Christmas dinner for the whole cast. The Provost Marshal had decided against any large groups. This was one time I was happy to go along with the MPs. However, Jerry, Peter, Les, and I decided to brave it over to the Ambassador's house and take care of the social amenities.

The Ambassador was most cordial, and amazingly cool, when you consider that his official residence is a prime target. The Ambassador told us that he had just received a report that they were bringing the casualties from Brink's Hotel into the Naval Hospital, and asked us if we'd mind going over to say hello.

It was a bloody mess. The wards and operating room

*Who said they're not drafting them like they used to. (NBC Photo by Frank Carroll)*

were swamped. Doctors from all over the city were working as fast as they could. I met one captain, a handsome kid from what I could see. A good part of his head was bandaged, as well as his right arm. We shook hands—left-handed. And he said, "I'm really embarrassed to meet you here, Mr. Hope."

"What do you mean, 'embarrassed'?" I asked. He shook his head sadly. "I'm the officer who was supposed to be in charge of *your* security. And look at me."

We walked into the ward that was being used as an emergency operating room, and I ran into one I'll never forget. He was lying face down on the table, and they were picking glass out of his back. He looked up with blood streaming down his face and said, "Merry Christmas." It wasn't sour apples, it wasn't a put-on. He meant it!

When we got downstairs and started to walk outside, there was an ambulance parked at the curb. I looked in, thinking there might be some kids in it. There was a priest, bent over the still body of what had been a young, vital GI just a few hours before. The priest turned, looked up at me, and said very softly, "At least for him all is calm tonight."

No matter where I am in the world, I always try to attend Mass on Christmas Eve. It's not because I'm Catholic, although when you marry one I guess you are whether you want to be or not. It's part of a pact I once made with Dolores. Actually, I don't remember agreeing to this. It must have been tucked in the marriage vows, somewhere between community property and having her mother come to live with us.

I gathered my covey of the faithful, Jerry Colonna, Barney McNulty, Jack Shea, Anna Maria Alberghetti . . . all those in need of absolution, and we headed out past the sandbag and barbed-wire barricades, through our Marine guards, to the magnificent cathedral, just two blocks away.

It was closed for the holidays. There had been an assassination on the steps just two weeks before.

We were directed to a small hotel just across the square. The priest heard confessions in the hallway, then he said Mass in a small room in the hotel. Not even a double room.

As we started back along the dark streets, after midnight, we heard footsteps behind us. There were three shadowy figures following us. We stopped and turned. They stopped and ducked into a nearby cul-de-sac. We continued walking a little faster. When we reached the next corner, there were the three guys waiting for us. We crossed to the other side of the street and hustled toward the hotel. We just about had made it when out of a dark doorway stepped the three guys again. This time they didn't hesitate. One of them walked right toward me. I put up my hands, he put up his. In it was a Bob Hope comic book which he wanted me to autograph. Laugh, I thought I'd die!

As we started up in the elevator, I realized I was starving. Shaking burns up a lot of energy. We all went up to the roof garden for a late snack. As we sat down to eat, we were joined by a lot of the war correspondents. One of them leaned over and grabbed my sleeve. He said, "Bob, you've got blood on your cuffs." It made a big headline for the UPI, but it didn't do a thing for my dinner. I got up and went down to my room.

I was exhausted, but somehow I didn't get much rest. Did you ever try to sleep with a parachute strapped to your back?

Before I went to sleep, I kneeled down to say my prayers. A voice from under the bed said, "Rots of Ruck!"

# CHAPTER SIX

Christmas '65 was a little more peaceful in Saigon. A truce had been agreed on, and it was comforting to know that, for thirty-six hours at least, killing would be illegal.

Due to the increase in population and the jams of civilian and military VIPs, we were unable to get reservations at the Caravelle Hotel. You couldn't get a room for money or hair spray; we tried both. Even the little white lizards who share the walls of your tropical suite were complaining of the overcrowding.

Most of the troupe stayed at the Meyerkord, a brand-new rest and recreational hotel put up by the military. The only rest and recreation was for the architect and the contractor. The Meyerkord is eight stories of solid crumble —our Government's first high-rise poverty pocket.

Maybe it's to fool the Cong. It looks like it's already been bombed. They had to rent a cockroach to keep up a front. They have the world's biggest laundry chute. It was supposed to be an elevator shaft, but there's no elevator. Well, you can't remember everything.

They charge you a dollar a night to stay there, and it's overpriced. Of course, the light sockets are very modern. If they ever wire them they're going to think seriously about ordering light bulbs.

Air conditioning? Forget it . . . they did. Hot water? Of course. Right there in the cold water tap. But I better warn you, it stops running as soon as you're soaped. It's kind of embarrassing. You have to run up and down the hall in your altogether trying to borrow a cup of water. And if you haven't seen our bandmaster, Butch Stone, in his altogether, you've missed a lot of altogether.

The military curfew was still in effect and none of the troupe were allowed out on the streets. But General Sternberg and his staff played the perfect host. They gave a cocktail supper on the roof garden of the Meyerkord. The "roof garden" was another figment of the architect's imagination. It was an asphalt roof with a superb view of the mortar fire and flares across the river.

Since there was no elevator and the "roof garden" was eight floors up, it meant that all the food and drink and plates and glassware had to be hauled up the center court by rope and pulley. It also meant our pooped group had to climb the eight floors, and most of them hit the sack early.

At five o'clock the next morning there was a tremendous explosion. The hotel shook. There was screaming . . . whistles . . . sirens . . . and running feet.

No, it wasn't the Cong. Just a detail lowering the plates and dishes from the "roof garden" to the main floor when a rope broke. But the sound effect was real, and when it comes to our crew, there's no shortage of hysteria. Here are a few of the reactions:

My able assistant, Sil Caranchini: "I threw myself under Johnny Pawlek's bed. At least I knew I'd be protected by a wall of human flesh."

Our veteran script gal, Joan Maas: "I counted my legs and when I got to two I ran."

Our imperturbable cameraman, Alan Stensvold: "I climbed into the film-changing bag. At the time it seemed like a good place to hide."

Patty Miller, our doll of a hairdresser: "My hair stood on end. I put on Joey Heatherton's wig and ran for it!"

Dick Collins, cool trumpetman: "I just turned over. I figured it was our drummer, Lloyd Morales, coming home."

Barney McNulty: "I was torn. I didn't know what to

save, myself or Bob's idiot cards. My decision is not for publication."

Our assistant director, Clay Daniel: "You'd be surprised the view you get from a chandelier."

I felt for these kids. Naturally they were nervous and upset their first time under fire. It's different for us old pros. I slept right through the blast like the true veteran that I am. Never even turned over. Of course, I was staying at a different hotel, the Astor.

I left the supper early to go and visit one of the greatest insurance salesmen of our time, the seventy-six-year-old Archbishop of New York, Francis Cardinal Spellman. Of course, he represents a pretty good company, Mutual of Vatican City.

This was his fifteenth annual Christmas visit to American troops serving overseas. He was staying at Ambassador Lodge's house, and I asked him if it would be all right if we took some pictures of him. He immediately agreed. I said, "I'm delighted to find that you're as hammy as I am." The Cardinal said, "Even more so, Bob. Remember, we want a big rating, too."

This holy man presented us with medallions for the entire troupe. When Jerry asked him if he would bless the medal, His Eminence said, "It's not a religious medal, Mr. Colonna, it's a token of my affection. You might say it's my advertisement." A delightful gypsy. When we left, he insisted on escorting us to our cars, in spite of the fact that he now has great difficulty in walking.

We attended Midnight Mass at the same soccer field that had been our show site that afternoon. The stage had been turned into an altar. There were two thousand American and Vietnamese, served communion by five priests. A choir of Vietnamese children sang. It was a soft, warm, starlit night, and Cardinal Spellman spoke of Christ and love and home and family, and for a moment that Christmas Eve there was no war. I fell asleep twice during the services

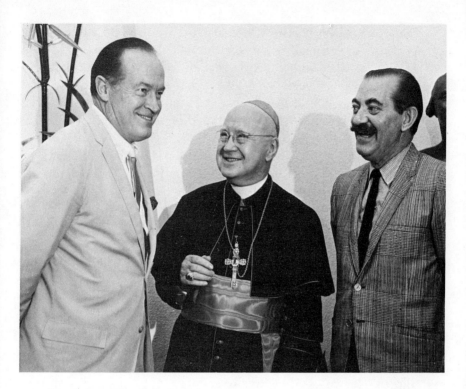

*"A joke's a joke, Bob, but please return the collection plate."* (*NBC Photo by Gary Null*)

and told His Eminence about it later, and he replied, "I know the feeling. I saw your act at Loew's State."

Just about every day you can pick up a newspaper and read about a skirmish taking place a few miles north of Saigon. They're usually referring to a base called Dian, which is French and pronounced Zee-on. (Don't ask me to explain it . . . I'm still trying to figure out some of the names Fernandel called me.)

Dian was to be the site of our next effort, so at 8:30 A.M. (dawn for people in show business) we stumbled out of the Meyerkord Hotel into a waiting convoy and raced for Tan

Son Nhut Airport, just outside Saigon. The run to the airport was uneventful, except for the fact that one car in the convoy smashed into a Vietnamese dirt carrier, a small cart pulled by a bicycle. The bike rider escaped unscathed, but if things run true to form, the ten shovelsful of dirt will probably wind up costing the U.S. around eight thousand dollars.

We were lucky. They have an interesting law in Asia that requires anyone killing a citizen in an accident to support his relatives for the rest of their lives. We have the same thing in the U.S. . . . It's called alimony.

The MPs accompanying the car were panicked because they had lost the convoy . . . and then, there's always the chance that it was some sort of a Cong trick to cause confusion or divert attention for a more lethal caper.

When we arrrived at the helipad, there were three big Chinook choppers waiting for us. We loaded them up one at a time, but all three took off together. I asked our pilot, Colonel John Lauterbach of Woodbury, New Jersey, about this, and he explained, "We always fly in two's or three's. If we send a single chopper out on a mission, Charley will shoot it down. When we travel in groups, they know they might get one of us, but we'll get them."

I took a look at the very determined machine gunners who peered out of each side of the 'copter. Their eyes never left the scenery and I didn't envy Charley below.

Flying north in our airborne jacuzzi we couldn't help marvel at the beauty of this lush jungle country. It was tough to realize that there was a war scheduled below . . . it looked so inviting. As I scanned the terrain with field glasses, I fully expected to see Little Caesar and Jungle Jim wrestling in the grass. They did not appear.

I did notice a lone observation plane flying low over the jungle below us. The gunner told me that this was a guy flying escort to draw any fire away from us. This really worried me. I've never asked or expected anybody to risk his life for me, with the exception of my tax accountant. Later I found out that this was standard operating procedure. They use the lone planes to try to get Charley to give away his position, sort of an aerial ambush. It used to work, but Charley is getting very sophisticated. He's not about to give up his beautiful hole in a rice paddy for one lousy observation plane.

Within the hour we were turning base leg for the helipad at Dian. This is the home of Major General Jonathan O. Seaman's scrappers, the First Infantry Division; an outfit the Cong tries to eliminate at least twice a day.

They're called "The Big Red One" and their motto is: "If you're going to be one . . . be a Big Red One."

Colonna and I had done shows for this Division back in World War II, so today we had to watch for sniper fire from both sides.

The size of the base is classified, but if I had been selling programs that day, I would have taken along about thirty-two hundred.

To keep the enemy off stride, there was no advance notice of our show playing the base, and when the news was passed by word-of-mouth, many of the guys thought it was some sort of a put-on. As one GI told me later, "Man, when they told me Bob Hope was arriving with a load of girls, I thought the General was on LSD."

The show site had been cleared of brush and trees a week before, ostensibly for the building of a ball field. The first game has yet to be played. I don't know what excuse they gave for building the stage. I guess the guys thought it was a pitching mound for midgets.

Just before the show started, I thought I might take a quick inspection tour of the rest room facilities. I inquired as to the whereabouts, and was pointed to a small tent in a clearing about a hundred yards away. There was a husky six-footer with a machine gun guarding the latrine. "Afraid it might run away?" I asked.

"I can't understand it. He's missed the mine field twice." (NBC
Photo by Gary Null)

In a Texas drawl that made LBJ sound like Rex Harrison, the guard answered, "It ain't nothin' to joke about, Mr. Hope. You be careful, because we draw sniper fire here twenty-four hours a day. We're not only surrounded by Charleys, but they's liable to be some in the audience."

And he wasn't kidding. They hire civilian crews to work on the base, and despite the fact that they are carefully screened, it's almost impossible to detect them all. They do find them out eventually, but it's usually a few lives too late.

Just then a sergeant major stepped to the mike and made the following announcement: "I want you men to keep the aisle clear on both sides of the stage in case of mortar attack. The left side of the audience will move out to the left and the right side will move out to the right. The center section will move out to the rear . . . and the cast of 'The Bob Hope Show' will take cover in those cozy foxholes immediately adjacent to the stage."

It's amazing how one little announcement like this can set the cast on edge. Carroll Baker ran into my dressing room and jumped into my arms. Or was it vice versa? Sometimes these details escape me.

Our fears were quickly alleviated when the security officer explained to us the elaborate precautions that had been taken. They had an infantry battalion of one thousand troops surrounding the base to prevent the Cong from lobbing mortars and lousing up my monologue.

In addition to the battalion there were four armed helicopters continually circling the perimeter of the camp with orders to shoot anything that moved.

As if this weren't enough to get me out from under my bunk, they have counter-mortar radar, which can detect a mortar in flight, track and compute its range and trajectory, and wipe out the source before they can fire a second round. I'd like to think this was all to protect me, but it wasn't so. When they've got three thousand GIs gathered in one place they don't take chances.

Actually, I didn't have to worry, for I had taken my own peculiar sort of precaution. I had persuaded my friend, the chubby disc jockey, Johnny Grant, to accompany us on the trip to Dian, for the sole purpose of using him as a shield. I figured with John's spread, I could save myself, the girls, and at least half the band.

This was Christmas Day and the whole cast really poured it on for these guys. The heat was blistering, and there was still another show to go, but Joey and Kaye and Anita and Jack stayed out on the stage until we had to pry them off. Subconsciously, everybody was trying to make it up to these fellows some way, and the weird part of it is, they don't ask for much. In Vietnam they're thrilled if they just wake up Christmas morning.

We did a lot of special Christmas material:

"In Saigon, Santa Claus doesn't have to slide down the chimney. He just waits and the building goes up.

"And Christmas dinner is really exciting here. Did you ever stick a fork in a turkey to see if it was going to go off?

"All the different battalions have their own Christmas displays, but they have to be careful. They found a manger scene yesterday with four wise men."

At the conclusion of the show, they presented me with a Vietnamese doll which bore the inscription: "This Is Your Oscar From The Officers and Men Of The First Division." I couldn't have been any happier if it had been a real Oscar for acting. It occupies a revered spot in my bedroom . . . right next to my Playmate Hot Water Bottle.

Before departing we had Christmas dinner with the troops in a tent. When we saw the spread that these guys had laid out for us, we all flipped. Here they had been living on rations for months in this malaria farm, and yet they managed to have turkey, crab, shrimp, cranberry sauce, candied yams, and two kinds of pie.

It's rather risky to put free food in front of actors. We piranhaed our way through those goodies and by the time the toothpicks were unsheathed, two of the cooks were missing.

It was kind of wild. Christmas dinner in a tent in the middle of no-man's-jungle, but strangely the spirit was there. Everybody was toasting everybody with glasses of purified Kool-Aid. Kaye Stevens was table-hopping all over the place, leading the community sing. Anita ran around with the Christmas menu, getting all the guys at her table to autograph it for her.

In the midst of the festivities, a young lieutenant rushed in very businesslike and announced, "Emergency, sir, we've got trouble at one of the outposts."

The Colonel jumped to his feet, "What's up?"

"I don't know how it happened, sir, but somebody goofed. Outpost Blue Fox didn't get its fruitcake."

That may not sound like an emergency to you, but a 'copter was airborne minutes later carrying fruitcake to Outpost Blue Fox. And in case that sounds overly sentimental, you'll be reassured by this story:

The day after Christmas a 'copter was hit by sporadic ground fire and the pilot, Lieutenant Bert Yancey, was saved, because he got hit in a piece of fruitcake he had in his pocket. I can vouch for the plausibility of this. I tasted the fruitcake. With my luck I'd have had a doughnut in my pocket.

We arrived at Bien Hoa around 3 P.M., and it was plenty hot. The temperature registered 98°. We don't know what the humidity was . . . the barometer had gone to the beach.

Bien Hoa is just outside Saigon, and about the only advantage of being stationed there is that you can get shot by a better class of people.

We did our show on a stage that had been constructed four days before for Cardinal Spellman—and the GI critics told me he was a smash. We worked to the 145th Army, the 173rd Airborne Brigade, the Royal Australian Regi-

*Two jokes later, he shot* ME! (*NBC Photo by Frank Carroll*)

ment, the 161st New Zealand Artillery Brigade, Vietnamese Air Force, Arvin troops (regulars of the South Vietnamese Army), and whatever Cong had managed to sneak in under the barbed wire fences.

All told there were seven thousand men in the audience. When we worked this base one year ago, there were only fifteen hundred men and the runway was a mass of wrecked 'copters and bombers. It was the first actual mortar attack on one of our bases and led to the escalation of our military in Vietnam.

I remember I had started out that show by telling the guys, "I've never seen such wonderful golfing country. Even the runway has eighteen holes." Then I looked out into the audience and spotted Colonna in a ranger outfit peering from behind a bush. I said, "I've never seen a tree with a mustache before. You there, why are you wearing that ridiculous outfit?"

And Colonna answered, "Supply Sergeant drinks. No, actually I'm an instructor in guerrilla warfare."

"You an instructor? Where did you learn to fight dirty?"

"Been married fifteen years."

Then he said, "I know I'm a fool to ask, but does it take much to be a guerrilla fighter?"

"No . . . just you and a mean gorilla."

That year we used Colonna in all different roles—a geisha girl, a Japanese soldier who still hadn't surrendered, Signal Officer on an aircraft carrier, and as Siamese twins. This year as a change of pace he worked in the medic sketch, did his whole act with the trombone, and sang three songs and worked with me. If you want to share our box lunches you really have to put out on these trips.

This year the sun really beat down on us. Just to make it even better, some well-intentioned work party had varnished the stage and turned it into a combination sun reflector and radiant heater. By the time the two-and-a-half-hour show was over, the band looked like it had been barbecued on a spit, and everybody wanted well done.

The heat really got to the girls. They were starting to peel off and spin like Migs. When Kaye Stevens came off, they had to catch her, and when Joey Heatherton finished her Watusi, they had to put ice packs on both her and the audience. When I came off, everybody rushed over and stood in my shade.

It really turned out to be an all-star show. A helicopter landed near the site and out stepped Martha Raye, Eddie Fisher and his pianist Eddie Samuels, folk singer Jackie de Shannon, and my old dancing pupil John Bubbles. Nobody with their kind of talent gets away with a fast hello. I drafted them on the spot and rushed them on stage.

Eddie showed up wearing a khaki jungle suit, a black leather holster complete with automatic, and smoking a cigar. He looked like a combination Trader Horn and Batman. He and Martha really broke it up on stage.

John Bubbles was worried. He wasn't sure he had the strength to walk out on stage, much less dance. Once he got out there working, we had to blow him off the stage with a Claymore mine.

John is beautiful, and what an act. He travels the world with tap shoes and a derby in a paper bag, and he's ready to go. And he's got life broken down into three simple categories: dancing, postcard writing, and sleeping. And sleeping is what he likes best. I remember one day when I found him dozing in the dressing room, I said, "John, you sleep more than anyone I ever saw in my life."

And John said, "I ain't sleeping. I just keeps my eyes closed cuz I don't want the world to see too much of me."

Two years ago in Turkey we were doing an ad lib soft shoe bit. I'd ad lib anything I could think of and John would follow like magic. He even made my stumbling look like it was part of the act. The audience dug it, and I guess

*"How would you like it if we shot back?"* (NBC Photo by Gary Null)

I got carried away. As we got to the wings, John mopped his brow and said to me, "Bobby—let's forget all that fancy stuff the next time. You may be auditioning, but I got it made."

John came up with a joke that we used everywhere for two years. After he finished his act, I'd come out and enjoy his applause and thank him. Then John would say, "Bob, before I go I'd like to ask you a serious question."

And I'd say, "Sure, John. What's on your mind?"

"Bob, do you believe in integration?"

"Yes, John."

"Well, then kiss me."

Now this might not be a big joke at a *Klan* meeting, but it sure broke up audiences all around the world. A year later I met Bubbles on the Johnny Carson "Tonight Show." I was there plugging a movie and John was there because he has talent.

He suggested we do our joke and the audience egged us on. We started out all right:

"Bob, I'd like to ask you a question."

"Sure, John."

Then, instead of his next line, "Do you believe in integration?", John asked, "Bob, are you against integration?"

Now, let me explain that when you work the same dialogue piece over and over, you don't usually listen to the feed line. I almost said the automatic "Yes" I was supposed to say, when an alarm went off in my head. I took John aside, and we had a conference on camera.

"Hey, John, you got the joke mixed up. You changed the feed line and we could've started a riot." John thought about it a minute, put the joke together mentally, and then said, "I wondered why that joke wasn't playing when I did it with Anna Maria Alberghetti." Then, and I still don't believe it, we started the joke over again and it broke up the audience. Bless them, bless them.

With that smorgasbord of talent at Bien Hoa, we were

*John Bubbles and a dancer that fakes it. (NBC Photo by Gary Null)*

almost an hour late on stage, and our security was getting very nervous. They hustled us back into the 'copters. The crew was striking the equipment as fast as possible, but security wasn't happy. Finally they got all loaded but our two veterans Bert Eason and Felber Maasdam. They were rushed out about forty-five minutes later. We figured our security was getting a little carried away until that night at General Westmoreland's party when we heard that the first place hit after the truce was Bien Hoa. Charley zeroed in the mortars and plastered the soccer field we had worked in. No casualties, thanks to the driving efficiency of our wardens.

In addition to being a superb strategist and diplomat, General Westmoreland is a delightful host. The first year he entertained our troupe his charming wife and family were there. Since that time all dependents were moved out of Vietnam and his family is now living in Hawaii. The General is batching it, but he threw a dinner for us that would have made Perle Mesta proud. There was enough food for Joey Heatherton, enough of the grape for Les, and a high chair for Stumpy.

He thoughtfully arranged a reunion between Anita Bryant and Army Captain Pete Dawkins. In 1958, Anita was the first Homecoming Queen in the history of West Point, and Dawkins, then one of America's most famous football stars and tops in his class scholastically, crowned her. Dawkins later went on as a Rhodes Scholar in England, and now is a ranger-adviser with the Vietnamese 1st Airborne Battalion.

Anita, with her sweet, innocent face and gentle manner, is one of the most successful medal thieves on the tour. She makes Fagin look like a choir boy. On our first trip she was given one of the Aussie "Go-to-Hell" hats, and a very nice kid gave her his marksman medal as a decoration. That started it, and since then the contest is on between the girls, and the trip is one vicious scavenger hunt—no holds barred.

To give you an idea, Anita smiled sweetly at the General and said, "My, that's the cutest little medal on your chest. I've never seen anything like it."

The General, not knowing he was being booby-trapped, explained that he and Vietnamese General Thieu had qualified together for their Airborne Jump wings. When they landed, General Westmoreland pinned his American wings on General Thieu, and in return the Vietnamese General pinned his wings on General Westmoreland.

And before the General knew what he was doing, he had pinned these wings on Anita. By the time we went in to dinner, our locusts had the General down to his stars. Kaye Stevens and Carroll Baker sat on each side of him. By the time he got up, he was a private. No wonder he made it to the top. There aren't many soldiers who can lose their good conduct medal in public.

One of our leading "Glom" artists from the year before was Jill St. John. She had more medals on her hat than Douglas Fairbanks, Jr., has on his pajamas. She was leading Anita fifty medals to forty-nine, but she met her Waterloo in the Officers' Club in Danang. She walked up to one very handsome captain, pointed to a medal on his lapel, and said, "Oh, that's an adorable one. What is it?"

The Captain replied, "I'm the Chaplain, ma'am, and that is a cross."

Jack Jones was very nervous at dinner, and when asked why, he said, "Well, I've been trying to get a call through to the States. It's extremely important that this message go through."

General Sternberg took right over. "I'll see if there's anything I can do." And, of course, when a General wants to do something, you can bet it's done. Five minutes later, Jack was escorted out to a phone in the hall to get his important message through. As with all phone calls in

*General Westmoreland trying to get Carroll Baker to re-enlist.*
*(NBC Photo By Gary Null)*

Vietnam, the transmission wouldn't have thrilled Don Ameche. Jack's voice kept getting louder and louder: "I love you! I love you! I said, I LOVE YOU!"

When Jack came back into the living room—there wasn't a sound. All conversations had stopped. He looked nervously around and then said apologetically: "Thank you, General, I think the message got through."

When we got back to Los Angeles, the object of his call, the beautiful actress Chris Noel, was at the airport to meet him. We all took one look and yelled: "We love you!"

As we rode back to the hotel, we were all a little beat and tattered, but we felt great. As they say in musicals, it was a most unusual day. And a most unusual Christmas. It would take Richard Rodgers to get me out of this.

# CHAPTER SEVEN

As an old house-counter from way back, I'd say that the biggest difference between our two trips to Vietnam was the size of the audiences for our shows. This trip a small base meant we were playing for five thousand men. The first year when they said a small base, they weren't kidding.

We played remote spots of two and three hundred men . . . the kind of bases where guys went to bed with their rifles by their sides; not for safety, but for companionship. Bases where the washboard doubled as the landing strip. If somebody stole their tom-tom they'd be out of communication with headquarters. When it came to plumbing, they were fighting a bush-button war with pull-chain equipment.

Two such bases were Vinh Long and Pleiku. Of course, we didn't know their names at the time. Before our first trip to Vietnam we were warned that all names, places, and destinations would have to be top secret; that they couldn't take a chance on any breach of security. We never knew where we were going, and the troops were never notified of the show until the last possible moment. In most cases they were not told who or what was appearing.

Yet, despite all the precautions, we seemed to be the only ones who were confused. Each night on the radio we could listen to "Hanoi Hannah," the "Tokyo Rose" of the North Vietnamese, and find out our exact destination, our time of arrival, our time of departure, and what time we should have our bags in the lobby.

*If I can't swing it, I use it as a cane. My trusty driver. (NBC Photo by Gary Null)*

It's sorta disillusioning, like watching your golf pro shank a simple wedge shot. Actually she gives our guys a lot of laughs. I hope she's never replaced by an Oriental rock 'n' roll group like Moo Gai Pan and the Egg Rolls.

On these smaller gigs, naturally, the facilities are kind of limited. There's no regular stage and we just work off the back of a truck. The fields are too small for the big planes, and that limits the number of people we can carry. We do a small "stand-up" show with the cast and our guitar player, Bobby Gibbons, standing in for the whole band.

When we took off for Vinh Long, we were told we were headed for Can Tho. At that time it really didn't make much difference, because none of us knew where either of them were. And if we had, we'd probably have canceled the trip.

We took off in a twin-engine Fairchild, which they had nicknamed the *White Whale*. And judging from the patches on it, it had been harpooned quite a few times.

There would be no opportunity for costume changes or makeup at the base. We were told to get in and move out in the shortest possible time.

Our gals came dressed in their show clothes, looking great, but a little overdressed for that hour of the morning. Linda Trainoff, our stunningly beautiful hairdresser, and Mike Moschella, our stunningly unbeautiful makeup man, worked on the gals en route. I couldn't help wondering what the Cong would think if they knew there was a flying beauty parlor overhead. I hoped they weren't too accurate with their ground fire. I was sitting on my best side.

We were cruising along at thirty-five hundred feet when I asked our pilot, Captain Kermit I. Cress, how high the Cong sharpshooters could reach. And he said, "Right now, with their 50-caliber machine guns, they can only reach about three thousand feet."

"That's cutting it a bit close, don't you think?" He just shrugged his shoulders and said, "We'll find out."

I noticed that the crew wore flak suits consisting of vests and pants. They were also using special seat cushions to protect them from potshots during landings and takeoffs. They told us that in the past they had been hit with everything, including a rusty 22-caliber rifle.

At that time they had just started arming the 'copters with heavier machine guns. A week before, one crew made an emergency landing and had to fight off the V.C. for

*I don't remember where it was, but it ain't Shea Stadium. (NBC Photo by Frank Carroll)*

cheers they gave me as the girls stepped off the plane, they were really starved for entertainment.

When we got off the plane, the first thing we saw was a sign that said, "Check All Weapons Here." I hoped that everybody had complied. One thing that doesn't thrill me is working to an audience with sidearms.

This was Christmas morning, and we played to 250 completely astounded and slightly bleary-eyed GIs. The company sergeant was a wreck. He'd been up since dawn, going from bunk to bunk yelling, "Everybody up! 'The Bob Hope Show' is arriving in two hours with a bunch of dames."

147

The exhausted GIs figured the poor sergeant was either bucking for a mental discharge, or that his jungle rot had attacked the brain.

The only reply he got which could be repeated in mixed company was, "Sarge, why don't you just surrender to the Cong and let us sleep?"

The kid who said it saw the show through the mess-hall window.

We opened the show with a lull. Our orchestra, Bobby Gibbons, was ready, but his amplifier wouldn't work. Thanks to the electronic skills of all the men there, we found the trouble. Someone had forgotten to plug it in.

I explained to the guys that our band was slightly reduced in size. Pointing to Bobby, I said, "That's all that's left of the band from the party last night. He's the square one. He only drinks napalm.

"Stand up and take a bow, Bobby. Not too far, I don't want you to black out."

I must say old Bobby, whose son is now on duty in Vietnam, did a great solo job backing all the acts. While we grabbed a quick lunch, a sergeant grabbed Bobby and rushed him off to give his wounded buddy a guitar lesson.

They turned on their tape recorder while Bobby sat in a steaming tent and played for the guys. Then he wrote out the chords so the guy would be able to play the tunes himself. He ended up giving the kid some guitar strings, his pic, and whatever music he had in his case. By the time he departed, all he had left was a case of sunburn.

The sergeant, realizing that Bobby hadn't eaten, scrounged up a can of beer and a bag of potato chips. Bobby didn't bother with the chips.

Sergeant Chris Shawn, of Gary, Indiana, who was stationed at Vinh Long, wrote an article for his hometown paper that was one of the greatest reviews our show ever got. Describing Vinh Long, he said, "Several times we watched our 'copters fire machine guns and rockets at Cong positions less than two miles away. At night lethal red tracer bullets whined over our barracks and explosions often rocked our quarters. It seemed like the last place on earth where they would send a big show like this.

"To wind up the show, Anita Bryant invited all us guys to join her in singing 'Silent Night.' It was the most emotional Christmas I've ever spent. I remember Janis Paige especially. She cried, shook hands with the guys and said over and over, 'No, *we* thank *you* for being here. We really do care.'"

Pleiku is so remote that Rand McNally had to ask Walter Cronkite where it was.

In case you should ever be looking for Pleiku, I suggest you take advantage of the wisdom of the pilots in the area. They all use a natural navigational aid. Just north of the strip is a hill called "Titty Mountain." . . . It's named after Homer J. Titty, who was the first man to plant flags on its twin peaks.

Pleiku is located about thirty-five miles west of Cambodia in the Central Highlands of South Vietnam. At the time we were there it was a strategic area for Charley. North Vietnamese troops were infiltrating down the Ho Chi Minh Trail to join up with the Cong troops. The mountains and ocean of jungle provided excellent hiding places. Units as large as regiments could maneuver without a trace beneath the vast cover of the rain forest. It was Charley's plan to occupy the highlands, cross to the ocean, cut South Vietnam in half, and throttle it with dispatch.

Camp Holloway at Pleiku was one of the reasons why the plan was to fail. It was located in the center of a magnificent plateau, a natural helipad. The air was so clear it reminded me of New Mexico or Arizona. (Sorry about that, California.)

At Pleiku we had, as the GIs call it, a small snafu. Which means, "Situation normal—all fouled up." Actually it means something similar to that, but a little less printable.

149

With all the decoy bases and rumors it was bound to happen. The 'copters containing our technical crew and Johnny Pawlek wound up going to the wrong base. When they didn't show up, we figured they had been shot down and put out an emergency alert for them. In the meantime, they were at a base about fifty miles away with a camera and a sound recorder all set up, a crowd of curious natives assembling, and they figured we'd been shot down. They sent out an alert for us. It was the closest I ever came to losing John Pawlek. I shudder to think what might have happened if the Cong captured him. He would have ruined half their golf swings and all of their sound equipment. The voice of Ho Chi Minh would today be just a whisper.

I'm ashamed of myself, picking on John. He's been with me for over thirty years. We both started together in knee pants. John is one of the oldest employees of RCA. He has also been there the longest. He started with the General back when the symbol of RCA was a Victrola with a dog sitting in front of it. And I'll say this for John: There's nobody who can make a dog sound more human, or vice versa.

We were welcomed by the base commander, Colonel John "Corncob" Hughes, so-called because he smokes a big corncob pipe and carries his tobacco in a sock. The last has nothing to do with his nickname . . . that's just where he carries his tobacco.

He's a twotime winner of the Distinguished Service Medal, and the men have the highest respect for him. Every chopper, Jeep, and plane had a corncob pipe painted on its side. On the radio, the code name of the tower is "Corncob Six." The poor guy couldn't quit smoking now if he wanted to.

While we were waiting for camera setup, the Colonel showed me all around the base (all four buildings), and pointed out the beautiful vista. I complimented him on the great view and the tremendous visibility, and he said,

"Bob, with the Cong hiding in the brush and our men sil-houetted on the plateau, we do not regard the visibility as an outstanding feature of this base."

I pulled an idiot card over my head and tried to pretend I wasn't there.

Just before the show started, he got all the cast together in our magnificent dressing rooms in the Base Operations hut. It was divided into men's and women's by an Army blanket, which at its supreme level was five feet high. We used the honor system. The girls promised not to look at me.

One of the great things about it was the washbasin with Jill St. John's name on it, and a note stating that the used water would be bottled and auctioned off after the show.

The Colonel said, "I don't want to alarm any of you, but of all the bases you've worked, this is the most dangerous.

"The Cong owns most of the real estate around here. We've got this little patch in the middle and we're not anxious to sell.

"Please do not wander off this area or we can't be re-sponsible for you. We don't have too much activity in the daytime, but with these monkeys you never know.

"If they knew we had all our personnel congregated in one spot, it would start raining mortars, so let's get the show started as fast as possible, and we'll try to get you out pronto."

In introducing me, Colonel Hughes said, "This guy has been doing this through the generation of your fathers and your older brothers . . ." At this point, I couldn't resist yelling from the wings, "Wait a minute, Colonel! It's me . . . not George Arliss!"

Never one to resist a sure-fire laugh, I borrowed a corn-cob pipe from one of the kids and walked out smoking it. I got a big laugh on the pipe and screams on my coughs.

I said, "This is great tobacco Colonel Hughes loaned me. He forgot to take the sock off.

"What's he got in here? I think he grows his own."

Everything played great. Those guys were so hungry for entertainment standing still would have played great. Sitting down would have been a smash. We tried to move the show, but with that kind of a house, you try and get any of our hambones off the stage.

While Jerry was out on stage killing the audience with "On the Road to Mandalay," Janis Paige wandered a few feet from the stage to grab a couple of fast pictures. Suddenly a voice from behind a bush said, "I wouldn't stand out here if I were you." It was a security officer assigned to watch for wandering actors. He informed her that a man had been picked off by a sniper in that very spot only two days ago. Inasmuch as she was standing with her good side toward the jungle, she quickly ran for cover.

It was here that we had our first encounter with the famed Montanyards of Vietnam—an independent tribe that inhabits the Central Highlands and dares the Cong or anyone else to set foot in their area. They're self-reliant and fierce. If they're on your side, you're lucky. If not, keep running.

The Montanyards are the last of the real isolationists. They hate the Catholics, they hate the Buddhists, they hate the lowlanders, they hate anybody who comes from the city, and they're not too sure about their cousins from the next village.

They're rough, tough, wiry little fighters who move through the jungle with incredible speed. Of course, they don't have a lot of clothes on to bog them down. They are dependent on no one, and are wooed by everyone. For they control the Highlands. It's their playpen and they're not anxious to share the building with anyone.

Fortunately, they took a liking to us and brought in their symphony orchestra which consisted of tom-toms, bones (which seemed vaguely familiar), and a thirteen-gong ensemble. It sounded like Stan Kenton out of Lawrence Welk

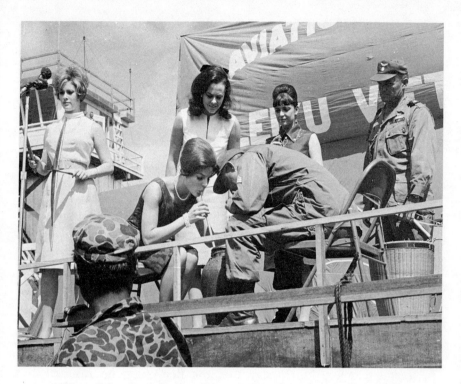

*Anita will hustle Coke anywhere. (NBC Photo by Frank Carroll)*

by Wingy Manone. At the end of their first number I scared the hell out of our crew by saying, "Thank you, men . . . thank you for that wonderful Good Humor music." They thought we'd all end up on the spit. But I guess the Montanyards were really auditioning for Hollywood, and they showed us the ultimate kindness—they insisted on initiating us into their Pleiku Friendship Club.

I was naturally quite excited until I heard they didn't have a golf course.

The ceremony consisted of drinking a potion, smoking a pipe, and being fitted with a brass bracelet. Normally, the potion is fermented rice wine with a dead rat floating in it. Sort of a jungle version of the martini. However, we were granted a special dispensation and allowed to fake it with warm Coke and a limp mosquito. This ritual made us blood brothers; we were now responsible for them and they were responsible for us. That's just what I needed . . . more relatives.

The potion was in a hollowed-out log, and we sipped it through long bamboo straws. It was supposed to make you big and strong. And if you survived it, you were!

They also presented us with crossbows and arrows which they had made themselves. (They do very little shopping at Sears.) Jill St. John insisted on trying hers out, and in doing so dropped the bow on her foot. No less than five doctors materialized out of thin air and began treating her. It goes to prove Einstein's theory that there is nothing like a dame.

The same thing happened when we got to Nha Trang. The foot was still bothering her, so Jill hopped over to the dispensary to get it X-rayed. The doctor was so gassed to see a real live movie star that the first thing he reached for was his camera. Twenty-four frames later, she started hinting for a little medical treatment. Instead, he rushed to a phone and called in another doctor, who in turn must have spread the word. Inside of five minutes, eleven doctors had arrived . . . all with cameras.

When they ran out of film, they managed to X-ray her foot and, fortunately, nothing was broken.

A reporter from one of the wire services, who had accompanied Jill to sick bay, looked rather dejected when he found out that nothing was broken and that he had no story. Jill, reading the message in his face, just smiled and said, "Maybe next time!"

Following Colonel Hughes' instructions, we wasted no time between the end of the show and our takeoff on the *White Whale.*

*Here we are—the road company of* Ship of Fools. *(NBC Photo by Frank Carroll)*

Once again their crew did everything possible to spoil us. Their steward, Sergeant Bernie L. McCleery, plied us with sandwiches and ice-cold drinks. In return, they asked us all to autograph the tablecloth. And, according to a letter we received from the pilot, Captain Cress, the tablecloth decorates the wall of the forward cabin to this day. Long may it wave.

The precautions of Colonel Hughes were well-taken. Three weeks later Pleiku was really hit by the Cong. A two-hundred-man force managed to infiltrate the perimeter of the base and got close enough to fire machine guns and lob mortars on the barracks. Their object was to cross the runway, blow up all the planes and helicopters, and set fire to thousands of barrels of rocket fuel in the ammunition dump.

In a matter of minutes, they managed to kill eight of our guys and wound another 125.

Bill Mauldin, the well-known cartoonist, was visiting his son, Bruce, a warrant officer, the night of the raid, and he gave us this account on our television show:

"I was awakened by machine-gun fire about two in the morning. The first round hit our hootch, killing two men and badly wounding a third. The kid was sort of holding himself together with two hands. He was in bad shape and I tried to get him to go down in a bunker with me, but he wouldn't move. He figured he was going to die, and the thought of going down into a hole didn't appeal to him. Colonel Hughes came in, saw what was happening, got us some help, and we put the kid on a mattress and carried him to the infirmary.

"All this time the mortar barrage and machine guns were blazing and the helicopters were exploding one after another. Only four choppers survived and they were airborne in a matter of minutes after the attack started. One of them crashed immediately, killing the pilot and injuring everyone else on board. They still don't know whether it was shot down or if it had been damaged on the ground."

According to Mauldin, "One of the big controversies is whether these people were local guerrilla fighters or professional soldiers from the North. This was a professional attack if I ever saw one. It was done with military precision and they retreated as a military unit. True local guerrillas could just have faded into the bushes. These birds, actually about a two-hundred-man force, were on the road. Our surviving helicopters caught up with them at nine o'clock the next morning and stayed after them for three days and chewed them to bits."

# CHAPTER EIGHT

The morning of December 26 found us winging our way to Cam Ranh Bay, about two hundred miles northeast of Saigon. Since there were no windows in our C-130 and the portholes were few and inaccessible, I got permission to sit in the cockpit so I could get a look at Vietnam from the air.

I did a take when I noticed that under the pilot's seat there was a gunbelt, revolver, and a mean-looking knife. I asked the pilot, "What do you need the knife for?" and he said, "Well, Bob, we peel a lot of potatoes up here." So I gave up on him and settled back to watch the scenery.

It was quite a sight. From twenty-five thousand feet, you could see a big hunk of South Vietnam. Just below us the land was flat, crisscrossed with hundreds of muddy streams woven in intricate patterns. To the east we could see the shoreline of the South China Sea. To the west was Cambodia and ahead of us to the north was the mountain range which more or less divides Vietnam. It all looked so quiet and peaceful, it was hard to believe that a vicious war was being fought in the rice paddies shimmering below.

But the reality of the war was inescapable. As we passed over Bien Hoa, just a few miles out of Saigon, we heard over the plane's radio reports of a V.C. attack, which fortunately was unsuccessful.

We made quite a landing at Cam Ranh Bay. None of that nice easy glide onto the runway. We literally dropped from the sky, diving straight down. I must say the pilot did

*Among friends. (NBC Photo by Gary Null)*

a brilliant job of landing, especially since I was sitting on his lap. When the plane finally stopped, I said to the pilot, "Did you ever work for Kamikaze Airlines? What kind of landing was that?" And he replied, "It's regulation around here, Bob. You've gotta come down fast . . . you can't expose yourself to the Charleys for too long."

I whimpered a little, put my shoulders back, made a mental note to look for my stomach at a more convenient time, and strolled bravely off the plane for my first look at Cam Ranh Bay.

Due to an exceptional configuration of land, Cam Ranh

Bay is one of the four best natural harbors in the world, perfectly protected from wind and typhoons and conveniently accessible to large ships.

For this reason, and because the Port of Saigon cannot adequately handle the enormous flow of supplies needed to support our men, Cam Ranh Bay has become one of the most strategic areas in the entire Vietnam operation and the scene of a massive buildup.

Before our guys arrived there, Cam Ranh Bay was nothing more than a vast expanse of sand. The only time it was ever used, at least in the last hundred years, was as a post for the French Foreign Legion. But all that sand was too much even for them, so they pulled up stakes and went somewhere else to forget.

We arrived in the midst of feverish activity. Everywhere you looked, docks, warehouses, roads, and airstrips seemed to be taking shape before your very eyes. Buildings were going up so fast, the termites were wearing safety belts.

Swarms of Army Engineers, civilian construction workers, and Vietnamese laborers were everywhere transforming the world's biggest sandpile into a port the size of Charleston, South Carolina. Everybody pitched in. I even met one chaplain who was driving a dump truck.

I didn't realize what a tremendous job was being done at Cam Ranh Bay until I heard we were spending over a hundred million dollars there. That's the reason why so many of our Congressmen and other VIPs have visited the Bay. They're thrilled to learn that there's a place in the world where American taxpayers are actually getting something for their money.

But despite all the construction, sand is still the big fact of life at Cam Ranh Bay, which I duly commented on in my monologue at the show we did there that afternoon for over six thousand troops:

"It's wonderful to be here on the moon; this can't be earth!

"I can't believe it. All this sand and no spinach.

"I've never seen anything like this place. It looks like a Texas cat box.

"This looks like a rest and recreation center for camels.

"It's sure a long walk between trees. They had a dog here . . . but he got psychoed out."

Another frustration for the men there is the fact that the cool, calm, green waters of the Bay, which would be so great to swim in after a hard day in the broiling sun and sand, are infested with sharks. So I also made a few references to this:

"I think I'll go for a swim after the show. I hope the PX isn't out of shark repellent.

"These sharks must be pretty hungry. I saw one of 'em eating in the mess hall.

"I didn't believe there were any sharks . . . till I found out there were three thousand GIs here named 'Shorty.'

"And don't you believe it when they tell you sharks will eat anything. We threw Colonna in . . . and they threw him back."

And so on. I was breezing along in my monologue when I suddenly heard a shot. Everybody in the audience jumped up and a lot of guys ran to their vehicles and roared away. My first thought was, "We've got to get better security—or better *writers*." Then, I thought this must be the start of a Cong attack. But I was wrong. What had happened was that a kid in the audience had accidentally pulled the trigger on his grenade launcher. But fortunately, nobody got hurt. I ad libbed, "Everywhere you go—Red Skelton fans," and went on with my monologue.

Actually, we had wonderful security at Cam Ranh Bay. Tough R.O.K. (Republic of Korea) Marines were stationed about a hundred yards apart on the perimeter around the show site. They were a very reassuring sight, silhouetted against the mountains.

The guards made us keenly aware of the possibility of

Cong in the area, which made some of us a little jumpy. Jack Jones made a comment on this situation that got one of the biggest laughs on the tour. Just before he went on, he called Les Brown aside and said, "Les, if the Cong attack, cut my *second* number!"

One thing happened at Cam Ranh Bay which was quite a switch—the GIs entertained us. Captain Allen Gardner of Lewisburg, Pennsylvania, treated us to a "free fall" exhibition which really had us gasping.

It really takes guts to fall thousands of feet and not pull the ripcord on your parachute until the very last second. I know *I* could never do it. I get nosebleeds just watching Wilt the Stilt.

As we watched Captain Gardner hurtling toward the earth, we were all subconsciously pulling the ripcord of his chute for him. The suspense was almost unbearable. It was like waiting for Pamela Mason to finish a sentence. Finally, after what seemed an eternity, the parachute mushroomed out over him. We all breathed a great sigh of relief and broke into spontaneous applause.

When he landed, Kaye Stevens, overwhelmed by the excitement of it all, rushed over to Captain Gardner, threw her arms around him, and gave him a big kiss. It turned out to be a mistake. She didn't realize that he still hadn't defrosted from his high-altitude leap, and it was like kissing the penguin in the Kool commercial. It took her about an hour to unpucker.

Later I interviewed Captain Gardner on stage and he turned out to be very quick with the ad libs. I asked him, "Do you have any control over where you land?" And he replied, "I landed right on the girls' dressing room, didn't I?" I said, "What were you thinking of all the time you were falling?" And he came back with, "I landed right on the girls' dressing room, *didn't* I?"

If there's anything I hate, it's a show-off who gets laughs.

After the show at Cam Ranh Bay, we boarded two giant

*Talk about your floating crap games. (NBC Photo by Gary Null)*

Chinook helicopters and about forty minutes later landed on the deck of the U.S.S. *Ticonderoga,* which was steaming slowly in the South China Sea about five miles off the coast of Vietnam.

The big choppers' landings on the deck of the *Ticonderoga* was rather exciting. Because they were going to take off again immediately, they kept their engines running and so the blades of the giant rotors continued to revolve, creating their own miniature hurricanes. We stepped off the choppers into a blast of wind that almost blew us back to Cam Ranh Bay! I haven't fought that big a wind since I stood next to Cassius Clay during a weigh-in. But scared as I was, in this moment of crisis, I didn't think of myself. My only concern was the girls' safety. So I grabbed Diana Lynn Batts and held her close to me until the choppers took off . . . and quite a while after that. But enough of my selflessness . . .

The guys were delighted to see us and gave us a very warm reception. But that was no tribute to us because being at sea so much of the time, they get even less entertainment than the GIs on shore. And let's face it, we were a welcome change from sea gulls.

Actually our visit to the *Ticonderoga* was sort of a surprise because originally we had been scheduled to appear on the U.S.S. *Enterprise,* the world's first atomic-powered carrier, which was also on duty in the South China Sea.

Strangely enough, we wound up on the *Ti* instead of the *Enterprise* as a result of a chance remark I made during a conversation with Ted Sally, a talented artist in North Hollywood who's done a lot of fine work for me through the years. Ted told me his son, Nick, was stationed on the *Ticonderoga* and I said, sort of casually, that we'll probably play it. I added, "In fact, I'd love to play the *Ticonderoga.* There's nothing like a nice, intimate flattop." I thought that would be the end of it. But apparently Ted had immediately cabled his son, saying: "Bob Hope would like to play the *Ticonderoga.*" Somehow, that message was relayed to Saigon and the wheels there evidently said, "Well, if he wants to play the *Ticonderoga,* I guess he must have a reason."

So there we were on the *Ticonderoga* with about a thousand pounds of idiot cards on which were inscribed a slew of hilarious jokes specifically designed for the *Enterprise,* an atomic-powered carrier.

In case you're ever booked to appear on an atomic carrier, these are still virginal:

"Nice to be here on our first nuclear aircraft carrier . . . I knew I was on a nuclear carrier . . . when the Captain shook hands with me, my nose lit up.

"I checked my wallet and my money was toasted.

"They say that the nuclear power on this ship has no effect on the crew. I guess it's just a coincidence that these four thousand guys all have curly hair.

"I've never seen a nuclear crap game before. . . . You just snap your fingers and the dice throw themselves.

"It's amazing the change that comes over a crew when you bring five beautiful girls aboard. We've got more atomic energy on deck than we have below."

Not that we were in any way disappointed being on the *Ti.* Although it's one of the oldest carriers in the fleet, it's still one of the most formidable fighting ships we have, and has done a magnificent job in the war in Vietnam. Despite its age, the Big *Ti* can still keep up with the younger ships. It's sort of the Cary Grant of the fleet!

Our stay aboard the *Ticonderoga* turned out to be one of the most unforgettable episodes in a trip that was replete with memorable moments. This was due to the fact that all the time we were aboard, the *Ticonderoga* was in action around the clock, its flight deck reverberating with the deafening roar of jets being catapulted toward Vietnam and then the ear-piercing whoosh and whine of their recovery as they returned from their missions. Everyone felt this

*The printer lisps.* (*NBC Photo by Gary Null*)

undercurrent of tension and excitement from the moment he stepped aboard the deck of the Big *Ti*. Although the war was just as real in Saigon, Bien Hoa, and Dian, there was an immediacy, a feeling of participation aboard the *Ticonderoga* that we got nowhere else.

We were officially welcomed by Captain Robert N. Miller, and I think he must have a writer stashed somewhere aboard. His opening line to me was, "It's great to have you aboard, Bob. You're the nicest thing that's happened to us since the last typhoon."

I had an answer for him but I restrained myself. I never try to top a man who has a load of five-hundred-pound bombs in his basement.

We were taken to our quarters, which were surprisingly comfortable considering the tightness of space aboard any naval vessel. Even the band, which doesn't often get the best of it when it comes to accommodations, did pretty well. They wound up in the sick bay, which actually was a big break because it was one of the few parts of the ship that was air-conditioned. However, Alan Stensvold and his camera crew weren't so lucky. They found themselves berthed directly under the steam chamber of the mighty catapult that shoots the planes into the wild blue yonder.

Next morning, I asked the bleary-eyed Alan how his quarters were. He said, "Oh it was just great, Bob. I dreamed I was the night watchman at Cape Kennedy!" I said, "Rough, huh?" And he said, "Well, to give you an idea, even my Timex stopped ticking!"

I could sympathize with him. Every time that catapult went off, you could feel it from one end of the ship to the other. It was like being aboard the U.S.S. *Mixmaster*. But Alan took it in stride because he's a hardy soul. After years of photographing me, there's very little that can shake him up.

That evening we were invited to dinner by Admiral Ralph Cousins, Commander of Carrier Division 9, and his

Executive Officer, Captain Willie House. The girls bombarded the officers with all sorts of questions about the carrier and Navy life in general. And strangely enough, the officers showed no reluctance at all in answering. Of course, I didn't have to ask any questions because I've played many carriers and know practically everything there is to know about them. Besides, we Hopes go way back in Navy history. My great-grandfather took part in one of the most heroic episodes in naval annals. When Admiral Dewey said, "You may fire when you are ready, Gridley!" it was my great-grandfather Gridley was aiming at! And when Admiral Farragut spoke those immortal words, "Damn the torpedoes! Full speed ahead!" it was my Uncle Sidney who held the idiot cards.

But as I was saying, the officers were really enjoying the girls' questions until Diana Lynn Batts came up with a lulu. She said to Admiral Cousins, "A ship this size must get awfully dusty. What do you do about keeping it clean?"

A look of disbelief crossed the Admiral's face. Then he looked over at me as if to say, "Bob, how would *you* like to answer this sweet child?" I did. I said, "That's no problem, honey. Once a month they run it through the carrier wash."

But while the talk was light and easy, there was an undercurrent of seriousness. Every so often, we could hear and feel the boom of the catapult and the roar of the planes. It became so insistent that the conversation began to lag. What was happening on the flight deck finally pushed everything else out of our minds. The Admiral, sensing this, suggested we all go up to the bridge and watch a squadron of F-8 Crusaders return from a mission over enemy territory.

It was eerie up there on the bridge. There was no moon and we were enveloped in inky blackness which lent a ghostly quality to the superstructure of the great ship as it pitched and rolled through the South China Sea. A thirty-knot wind whipped at us and we had to hang on to the rail to keep our footing. Any moment I expected Boris Karloff to tap me on the shoulder and whisper, "Come . . . I need you in the laboratory"!

The few dim lights visible only added to the nightmarish scene. They were the runway lights along the flight deck which served as a guide for the returning planes.

As we watched, hypnotized, a plane streaked in out of the darkness, picked up the beam, and landed with amazing accuracy in the narrow strip of flight deck they call "the slot." Its tail hook grabbed the arresting wires, and the plane screeched to a sudden stop. It was immediately pulled away from the landing path to make room for the next plane.

Recovery is a tricky, dangerous operation even in the daylight and under favorable circumstances. At night, with the ship pitching and a small gale blowing, it seemed to us an incredible feat, like riding a skateboard in the fast lane of the Hollywood Freeway. Yet these pilots perform this intricate maneuver day in and day out and consider it just part of the job.

Another plane landed. Then another. Then the next plane picked up the beam, and started its approach. We all sensed immediately that something was wrong. Its angle of descent seemed somehow different than the others. The undercarriage of the plane scraped the stern of the carrier with a sickening sound, its hook missed the arresting wires, and it hurtled across the deck and crashed into the sea in a ball of flames.

It all happened so suddenly and so fast, the full impact of it didn't hit us immediately. For a second or two, everyone was stunned. Then the ship's siren pierced the air and electrified the crew into action. From everywhere, men poured out onto the deck and rushed to the spot where the plane had disappeared into the sea. Many of them threw their lighted flashlights into the water to pinpoint the spot.

After a few heart-stopping moments, a triumphant yell

*Arnold Palmer or Betsy Palmer? (NBC Photo by Gary Null)*

went up. Someone had spotted a parachute floating a short distance from the ship. But the elation was short-lived. The pilot was nowhere to be seen.

Tension became almost unbearable. I heard a sound behind me, looked around, and saw Joey Heatherton sobbing uncontrollably. Kaye Stevens was hanging on desperately to an officer's arm, her face registering shock and disbelief. And to tell the truth, I felt pretty weak myself. I had the strangest feeling that my knees were made of Kleenex and would buckle under me at any moment.

Then a great cheer went up. Word had just come that the

pilot had somehow managed to eject from the doomed plane and had been picked up about a hundred yards astern by one of our support ships, the destroyer *Turner Joy*.

He was Lieutenant W. S. Braugher, of Newark, Ohio. He was alive and in good shape. We all breathed easier, although we didn't stop shaking for quite a while.

Later I dropped in to see Lieutenant Braugher in the sick bay on the *Ti* where he'd been taken after his dramatic rescue. I said to him, "That was pretty good. Now what are you gonna do for an encore?"

He smiled weakly. He was still in shock from his close call. "Anyhow," I added, "I can't tell you how glad we all are that you decided to stick around for the show."

Later that night, we heard the voice of the Chaplain over the P.A. system conducting the "Lights Out" prayer, giving thanks for the miraculous rescue of the pilot. I was moved by the great reverence with which this prayer was received throughout the ship. At its close, we all whispered a heartfelt "Amen."

I was so charged up with the excitement of the dramatic incident that I just couldn't sleep so, around 2 A.M. I finally gave up, dressed, and went on deck. I thought I'd find it deserted, but it was a beehive of activity. Our supply ship, the *Sacramento,* was alongside unloading an incredible variety of items, ranging from cans of beans to five-hundred-pound bombs.

The *Sacramento* is the largest supply ship in the U. S. Navy. It carries food, water, fuel, and ammunition for the entire Seventh Fleet. It's sort of a huge, floating A & P. It was fascinating to watch the tons of food disappear into the vastness of the *Ti*'s hold.

I found out an interesting thing about the bombs. These five-hundred-pound babies are attached to the planes by powerful magnets. Once over the target, the bombardier releases the bomb by switching off the magnets. However, every once in a while something goes wrong and the bomb is not released. The plane then has to return to the carrier with the bomb still attached.

As I've said, landing a plane on the postage-stamp-size deck of a moving carrier is tricky at any time. With a live five-hundred-pound bomb hanging precariously from your plane, it's about as easy as stealing a wallet from a nudist. It calls for the delicate touch of a safecracker, the timing of a Willie Mays, and the guts of a kosher pastrami salesman in Cairo.

And I thought I lived dangerously when I was in vaudeville!

I asked one of the pilots, "What happens when a bomb gets loose while you're landing, and drops off?" He said, "It used to be a bit of a problem, but no more. Now the flight deck is angled, so when a bomb breaks loose, it just rolls off the edge."

"I said, "Uh huh. But what if it *doesn't* roll off?"

He shrugged and said, "Then *we* go over the edge."

I persisted. I said, "Has it happened recently?"

He looked me right in the eye and said, "Let me answer you this way, Bob. When we left port, this ship was twice as long!"

I hope that guy re-enlists for another hitch. Who needs the competition?

Thanks to the happy ending to what could easily have been a disaster, we were all able to relax aboard the *Ticonderoga* the following day, and take advantage of the facilities aboard ship which were unavailable in Saigon. In Saigon, the musicians and technical crew had stayed at a transient GI billet, euphemistically called a hotel, where the water was undrinkable, the showers just teased you with an occasional trickle, and where the air conditioning consisted of a few broken windows. The fellows called it the "Bowery Hilton," among other things.

Consequently, the *Ticonderoga* with its hot showers,

laundry service, and food that was actually edible seemed as luxurious as the *Queen Mary*.

The band spent so much time under the showers, they sloshed for days. The laundry service was especially welcome. We move so fast on these trips, there's never any time to get it done, and it gets to be a problem, especially in that heat. In fact, next year we may leave one musician home and take Katy Winters instead.

Laundry service aboard the *Ti* was fast, and it came back clean, but it will never get an award for neatness. Instead of being ironed and folded, my laundry came back in one big lump. I couldn't figure out why my shirt felt so tight, until someone asked me, "How come you're wearing a tie with your jockey shorts?"

Another amenity aboard the *Ti* was closed-circuit television. The programs were mainly reruns, ball games, and old movies, but to the sailors it was a most welcome diversion during their off-duty hours. After you've been at sea for six or eight months, even Charlie Chan looks good.

They really showed some vintage movies. I saw one war movie that was so old, John Wayne played the part of a coward. Not only that, Erich von Stroheim was on *our* side.

I didn't realize how old some of those movies were until one sailor asked me if I could get him Pola Negri's autograph. I promised him I'd check with Bing.

But I'm sure none of the men watched TV that day. The big item on the agenda was girl-watching. In fact, the girls practically took over the ship. Each of them was "assigned" to a squadron and an escort officer, who conducted them on a tour of the ship. To qualify as an escort, you had to be a bachelor. This turned up a most unusual statistic. Among the *Ticonderoga*'s crew of five thousand, there wasn't a single married man.

They drew lots to choose the five escorts. I didn't watch the drawing. I hate to see 4995 men cry.

The girls created quite a stir when they came on deck.

Carroll Baker really had the fellows bug-eyed. She was wearing a gold lamé outfit that looked as though it had been sprayed on, with skin-tight toreador pants, and gold shoes with five-inch spike heels.

As she stepped onto the deck, four pilots took off . . . without their planes.

One sailor looked at her and said, "Miss Baker, I think you're in big trouble."

Carroll said, "How do you mean?" And he said, "You're wearing more gold than the Admiral!"

When the gals agreed to go on a tour of the *Ti*, they didn't realize what they'd let themselves in for. Below decks there are miles of corridors and passageways. After about an hour of hiking, they began to wilt a little. Kaye Stevens turned to her escort and said, "I'm pooped. How long *is* this ship?" And he said, "I'm not sure, but the other end is in Okinawa!"

Joey Heatherton said, "Y'know, it'd be awful if we got lost down here. They wouldn't find us for days." And her escort, a Navy man to the core replied, "Yeah, how about that?"

But the girls got back O.K., and not a moment too soon, because they had to get ready for the show that afternoon and you men know how long it takes a woman to get ready.

Like all married couples, Dolores and I have often quarreled because of those seemingly endless waits before leaving the house for a dinner date.

But after years of this, we've reached a wonderful compromise, and no longer fight about it. Dolores now just waits patiently till I'm ready!

To get ready for the show, the girls requisitioned the officers' wardroom and turned it into a beauty parlor. It was something you had to see to believe. There they were, aboard one of the mightiest battleships in the fleet, sitting under hair dryers, applying mascara, manicuring their nails,

*Joey Heatherton conducting a deep-breathing exercise. (NBC Photo by Gary Null)*

and doing the hundred and one things girls do to make themselves "beautiful." It was as incongruous a sight as seeing Dean Rusk at the Pink Pussycat *East*.

I don't have to tell you that this operation attracted hundreds of guys from all parts of the ship, who watched the girls' every move with utter fascination. The girls enjoyed all this attention but I found it a little annoying. I hate to sign autographs while my nail polish is drying.

A lot of people ask me why I carry a golf club in my hand on these trips. And I tell 'em, "I have to carry it . . . it's growing there." Actually, I'm like all the rest of the golfers. I keep swinging a club all the time, hoping I'll find "the secret." For Billy Casper it's elephant steaks, for Al Geiberger it's peanut butter sandwiches, but for me it's still a mystery.

Billy Casper took his own food with him when he went to Vietnam. He was doing fine until his lunch bit him. Billy's a member of the buffalo meat for lunch bunch. It includes him and Hugh O'Brian. Casper is a living testimonial to buffaloburgers. He's the only pro in the tour who travels with a caddy and a game warden.

I try and sneak in a couple of holes of golf any time, any place I go. But I never figured to play on an aircraft carrier. So I was pretty shocked that morning when Captain Willie House, the Admiral's Exec Officer, hustled me into a corner and said, "Would you like to hit a few?" Well, as it turned out, he's as frustrated a golfer as I am, and he had hidden on board a bucket of beat-up golf balls. I hate to say it, but our Exec Officer was another one of those fellows who never leaves a driving range without one of their balls in his pocket.

We got on the pitching, rolling flight deck (you'll notice I established my excuse before I hit a shot) and started teeing up the balls. My opening line was, "Stand back—this is the first time I've ever shanked an ocean. I've seen water holes before, but *this* I gotta report to *Sports Illustrated*."

That was the last line I had, and the last one I needed. In no time at all we had a gallery of five hundred sailors who turned it into an ad lib insult contest. The kindest remark was, "Bob, you've got a stance like Sam Snead, a backswing like Arnie Palmer, and a follow-through like Ben Hogan. But somewhere along the line, Hermione Gingold sneaks in!"

And Gold Braid didn't help our Exec Officer. He came in for his share of the insults, too . . . especially when he lifted his head and took a divot in the deck. We had a great half hour on deck with the verbal slings and arrows flying back and forth among all the guys, and a free-for-all picture-taking and autograph session.

And I can hardly wait to go to Captain Willie House's court-martial and hear him explain what a golf divot is doing on the flight deck of the carrier *Ticonderoga.*

I must take a minute here to pay tribute to the Captain and crew of the *Ti* for the remarkable lengths they went to in helping us put on our show.

We were filming the show in color so lighting was a big problem, especially in the case of the girls. Filming aboard a moving ship, the problem is intensified because the light is never constant. Cross lighting is very unflattering to girls, but "kind" to men. It makes men look more manly but it gives girls harsh lines. The wrong lighting can make Liz Taylor look like Walter Brennan!

The only way to overcome this dilemma was to use the sun as the "key light" and steer the ship so that the sun always hit it at the proper angle. The men on the bridge really understood our photography and lighting problems. Precisely at one-thirty, as the music was being set up on stage before the start of the show, they turned the huge ship around and cut the speed down to five knots so that not only was the sun just where we needed it, but the smoke from the stack was blowing out of camera range. They held the ship steady for us and followed the sun westward as the hours advanced so that we had perfect lighting all through the show. How's that for cooperation? Thanks to this fantastic job of seamanship, we got conditions comparable to those we have at NBC in Burbank.

The girls were especially grateful. They considered it the greatest act of chivalry since Fat Jack Leonard gave up his seat in the subway to a troop of Girl Scouts.

We did the show for about thirty-five hundred men who not only jammed the deck but watched it from every possible vantage point. Some were perched precariously on the superstructure high above the stage, some crowded onto planes, and there was an added audience, the men of the destroyer *Turner Joy* steaming nearby, who listened to the show on the ship's radio and watched through binoculars.

The men on the *Turner Joy* really dug the show. After it was over, they sent the following message: "Please relay to the Hope troupe, Miss Baker, Miss Heatherton, Miss Bryant, Miss Stevens, and Miss U.S.A. Although we have the ultimate in back row seats, the very thought of the nearness of you has done wonders for our morale. Thank you."

In my monologue, I regaled the boys with jollies like these:

"It's wonderful to be here on Catalina Island. Well, don't stare. . . . that's what they told me to get me here.

"What a monster! I didn't know Texas would float!

"Isn't it amazing what you can rent from Hertz these days?

"But this ship really is a beauty. I understand half the whales in the Pacific are trying to get her to go upstream.

"This carrier's so big, you can go over the hill without leaving the ship.

"If you get seasick, you need a two-week leave to get to the rail.

"But big as it is, it's very easy to handle. It can turn around in either the Pacific or the Atlantic.

"It's a thrill to be here on the U.S.S. *Crapgame*. . . . Why kid around . . . I know your *real* mission.

"I've never seen such action. I never heard of a chaplain wearing a green eyeshade before.

"What gambling! The Navy had to buy the ship back three times last month.

"Coming in for a landing on this carrier is so tricky, you've got to get shot down to land safely."

We did a long show, it ran for about three hours, and I enjoyed every minute of it. But then, I've always enjoyed working on carriers. There's the audience on deck, surrounded on all sides by a shark-infested ocean. Like me or not, they've got to stick it out. It's the kind of audience I love, thirty-five hundred captives!

I know nobody walked out on me. I'd have heard the splash.

After the show, Carroll and the rest of the girls were invited by its skipper, Captain Nicholson, to go aboard the *Sacramento*, our supply ship, cruising nearby. Captain Miller of the *Ticonderoga* objected. He didn't like the idea of his ship being deprived of the girls' company. Whereupon Captain Nicholson threatened to cut off the *Ti's* food supply for a couple of weeks, so Captain Miller quickly gave his O.K. It was a heartening example of the co-operation between the ships in our Navy and a stirring testimonial to the power of blackmail.

The girls were flown to the *Sacramento* by helicopter and shown through this huge floating warehouse. They also witnessed the promotion of two ensigns to lieutenant junior grade. The two new officers received an unexpected fringe benefit when they were kissed by each of the girls. I hope they took a picture of this touching scene. It would make a great recruiting poster.

On the *Sacramento* the girls really outdid themselves

in the souvenir-snatching department. By the time they left, they'd collected so many medals and insignia, you couldn't tell the Captain from a messboy. Joey Heatherton's collection was really a sight to behold. She had so many medals, bars, eagles, and assorted fruit salad that if she ever quits show business she can always get a job as a doorman at the Savoy Hotel.

Of course, being a star, I don't indulge in such childish pursuits as collecting trivia. It doesn't fit my image. Just the same, I wound up with a few very choice momentos, real treasures: an egg roll tossed through the window of the American Embassy in Saigon by a nearsighted Viet Cong; a hubcap from General Westmoreland's command car stolen by a six-year-old Buddhist during a Little League anti-government demonstration; and rarest of all, the stuffed remains of the water buffalo that accidentally bumped into John Wayne on his visit to Vietnam.

That evening, after dinner in the officers' wardroom, there was such a feeling of conviviality and warmth that almost without knowing it, we found ourselves putting on an impromptu show. Carroll Baker surprised everyone with a version of "Playmates" in which she showed a remarkable flair for comedy. She was followed by Jack Jones and the other members of the cast doing bits from their nightclub and personal appearance acts. It was all very spontaneous and relaxed and wonderful fun. As a "finale" I thanked Captain Miller and everyone aboard the *Ti* for their hospitality and kindness to us.

It was a heartwarming finish to our exciting stay on the *Ticonderoga*. I know it was an experience that will stay with all of us for a long, long time.

# CHAPTER NINE

We awakened in the morning to the hiss of steam and the shock of the catapult as the bombers took off on the flight deck above us, headed for North Vietnam. Our departure had to be a matter of split-second timing. Thirty minutes after the last bomber was launched, the first flight would be back in the landing pattern, and they didn't have enough fuel to loiter. Our 'copters would have to be off the deck in a matter of minutes.

There was a twenty-five-knot wind across the deck as we raced to our Chinooks. Their rotors were already turning. There was no time for social good-byes on the front porch. So here and now, in behalf of our troupe, I'd like to make our bread-and-butter thank-you's to the officers and men of the *Ticonderoga*. She may not be the fastest carrier in the fleet, but when it comes to hospitality she makes the Beverly Hilton look like a flophouse.

Once aloft we opened our sealed orders and found out that "Hanoi Hannah" had been absolutely correct the night before on the radio. Our destination was An Khe, a new base carved in the strategic Central Highlands, an area which had been completely dominated the year before by the Cong. It's the home of the world's most mobile division, the 1st Cavalry (Airmobile), or, the First Team, as its men proudly call themselves.

When the First Team moved in it was solid jungle. The division's Assistant Commander, Brigadier General John M. Wright, took a machete and led his men in to clear the area by hand. Today there are sixteen thousand men

*On this course all the traps are boobied. (NBC Photo by Gary Null)*

there, and 480 helicopters, which makes it the largest concentration of men and machinery in Southeast Asia since the French split for DeGaullesville in 1954.

As we descended toward the helipad we got our first good look at "The Malaria Capital of the World." It's the kind of place that a rock python might take his wife for the weekend. But she wouldn't like it.

We were met by Major General Harry W. O. Kinnard, Captain Henry Thorpe from Columbus, Georgia, the only surviving officer of his company from a fierce battle at Ia Trang Valley, and by a color guard of mosquitoes.

I'd seen lots of mosquitoes in my time, but these kids had tricycle landing gears. They were so anxious to dip their snorkel in your bloodstream they used to tiptoe up behind you and bite you in the ankle. They were really huge. If they couldn't get your blood, they'd lean on you.

An Khe is a beautiful setting for a war . . . a panorama of lush, green, rolling hills and mountains, broken only by huge poles with attack sirens circling the perimeter of the base. Under the circumstances they were a comforting sight.

The men call the village of An Khe "Gunsmoke." Possibly because of the TV show, and the fact that it reminds them of home. They also call it "Happy Valley" because more V.C. are killed here than any other place.

Like just about every outfit we met in Vietnam, these guys are doing a hell of a job. It's incredible to think in the middle of this jungle they're operating the largest heliport in the world.

They can airlift artillery battalions with their "Flying Cranes"—huge, strange-looking helicopters that resemble a berserk praying mantis. They can lift bulldozers and downed helicopters to be brought back for repair. They can support an army—they can deliver an army, and they can attack an army. As one French correspondent said, "Ah, but if only we had had the helicopters. They are the difference."

The First Team hates to come back from a run empty-handed. A few weeks prior to our visit, spotting a village in trouble, they swooped in and rescued a Vietnamese Catholic priest while the V.C.s were desecrating his church. He promised them that he and his people would pray for the gallant men of the 1st Cavalry.

At An Khe the Viet Cong activity is heavy and constant. Every night some part of the area is tested by Charley. In fact, the perimeter of the base was only 150 yards from the show site. And we were, theoretically, within mortar range. But as usual, thank God, we were up to our idiot cards in security. The entire area had been bulldozed to eliminate any possible cover for snipers. They had a screening force out beyond the perimeter of the base, and small observation aircraft and armed choppers in the air at all times.

As we made our way to the show site, it was muggy with an occasional light sprinkle. The ground was wet and muddy. We crossed a small footbridge which bore a sign reading: "Constructed for Miss USA." Hanging on the other side was a pair of boots with my name on them. There is some sort of symbolism here, but I'm afraid to figure it out.

The 1st Cav certainly rates number one when it comes to ingenuity. For the girls' dressing room they had a big Chinook helicopter parked right next to the stage. They equipped it with mirrors, chairs, makeup tables, the works. For the fellows, the arrangements were not quite so fussy. We had a tent, a can of Raid, and monogrammed mosquitoes.

Show time was 10:50 A.M.; at home I don't have my hypodermic of coffee before noon. But it's amazing how an audience like this can get you up. We had over ten thousand troops, including Army, Air Force, and a small group of nurses in green fatigue outfits. I know Givenchy wouldn't approve, but out here in the jungle they looked like the most beautiful high-fashion models.

We had to follow some pretty rough competition. In the weeks preceding our visit, the men of the 1st Cav had played host to Kathy Nolan, Western singer Roy Acuff, Martha Raye, Secretary of Defense Robert McNamara, and Cardinal Spellman.

During the show we could hear mortar fire in the distance. We were told that there was a strike a few miles from the site. Later, we received word that two men had been killed in action during the show. Not far away was Mang Yang Pass, where four thousand French soldiers

*Everything in this picture is well built. (NBC Photo by Gary Null)*

lost their lives. This pass is also known as "The Street without Joy."

General Kinnard came down from the action in the jungle to open the show. I think he had a writer up there in a foxhole. He said, "The reason they picked me is because I'm the only man in the division old enough to remember when Bob Hope started doing this."

And then he cautioned the guys, "I understand this thing is going to be televised. So if the camera swings your way, I want you to be laughin' and scratchin'." Where was the General when I was working the Stratford in Chicago?

The General didn't have to worry about the audience . . . they were great. Naturally, at An Khe we talked about the 'copters:

"We have a lot of Army 'copter pilots in our group today. First time I've played to an audience that shook before I did my act.

"We can all be proud of these men in the airborne Watusi.

"It takes a lot of courage to head into combat in one of those cockamamie hair dryers.

"They're doing a great job of medical evacuation. If you're not wounded when you get on, they shake something loose for you."

One of Jack Jones' first big record hits was a song called "Wives and Lovers." The audience yelled for it every place we went. Jack Jones had made a few appearances on our show and from the frantic reaction of the younger set, especially in my house, I knew he had to make the trip with us. Funny thing about my kids—they go to jello at the mere mention of somebody like Jack Jones, and yet I can wander around the house day after day virtually unnoticed. I'm gonna have to get a bigger star for my pajamas.

At An Khe he plucked a lovely young Army nurse from

*Jack Jones giving first aid to one of our Florence Nightingales. (NBC Photo)*

the audience to do the number with him. Her name was Sharon Ferrari, she was from Antelope, Oregon, a graduate of the University of Portland School of Nursing, Class of '64, and she was an absolute natural. When the lyric asked, "Are you ready for love?" she ad libbed, "I'm ready, I'm ready." And when the lyric suggested that the wife should "Wear something pretty," Sharon just looked down sadly at her fatigue outfit. The audience dug it all, and of course this was a number we had to use on the television show.

Following Jack's tremendous ovation, I called Specialist 4th Class Brian H. O'Connell of Studio City, California, up on stage. I wish you could have seen the look on Brian's face as he walked toward me. The poor guy didn't know what to expect. Just before we took off from Los Angeles, his wife ran up to me with a picture of his twins that he had never seen. She asked us to deliver the picture to Brian which we did—on stage.

It was one of those strange moments that can only happen in a war. A kid—a father—standing in the middle of a jungle, eight thousand miles from home, looking at a picture of his kids—seeing them for the first time. We were all so emotionally moved we were torn between laughter and tears. And not knowing what to do, we all started applauding. And, that day at least, the O'Connell twins had ten thousand godfathers.

Just before the finish of the show General Kinnard made a very nice thank-you speech in which he inadvertently harpooned me. He was trying to think of some way of expressing how he felt about the show, and the tremendous cast we were lucky enough to have, and he said, "Bob, even without you this would be a great show." I turned and gave him the Jack Benny stare number three. And then it just slipped out. I said, "General, may I say the same about your outfit." That started a howl that must have shaken a few Cong out of the trees.

*This is Specialist 4th Class Brian H. O'Connell with a glazed look just after I showed him the first picture of his newly born twins. (NBC Photo by Gary Null)*

We closed by singing "Silent Night," with the guys joining in. During the song, Diana Lynn Batts really broke down and bawled. Later, in the chopper, she asked Peter Leeds, who has made all the trips, how it was humanly possible to sing to these men without breaking down. Peter replied, "Just look over their heads. If you ever look into those faces, you're dead."

Our supper show was scheduled at Nha Trang, in peacetime a beautiful resort on the coast of the South China Sea. Our flight took the better part of an hour. About ten miles out, the chopper started descending and turning in an arc. Natch, the girls were alarmed, and I explained suavely that the pilot was taking evasive action to avoid enemy fire. Just then the pilot announced that he was dropping down so we could get a good look at the Miami Beach of Southeast Asia.

From high up in our shaker the soft blue waves rolling up against the gleaming white sands of the beach looked great. The only thing that marred it were the miles of barbed wire and the foxholes with the sentries on guard.

As we banked in over the beautiful harbor we could see the picturesque French colonial houses with sculptured hedges, the restaurants, bars, and the many shops in town. It's no wonder that both sides have picked this almond-eyed slice of the Riviera as their rest and rehabilitation center. As the saying goes, "Nha Trang belongs to the Americans and Vietnamese in the daytime and to the Cong at night."

Nha Trang is the headquarters of our green beret boys, the Special Forces men whose work has become part of our national folklore in song, and now even in the comic strips.

The Green Berets are worthy contenders for the Superman and Batman image. These superbly trained men are all specialists in some field: medicine, engineering, demolition, weapons, or communications. And they are all experts at making friends. It has been said that in the

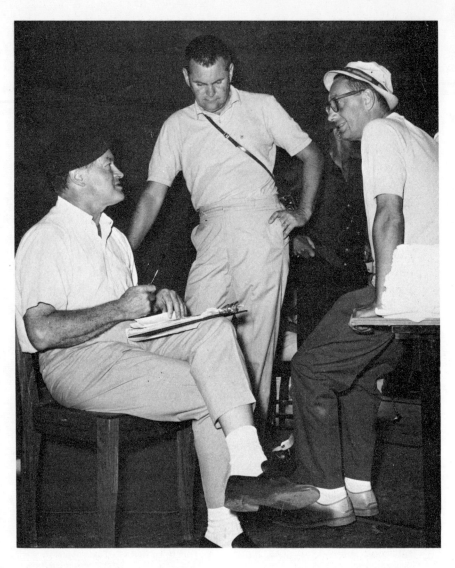

*My writers Mort and Bill pleading for a three-year pass. (NBC Photo by Gary Null)*

end the battle in Vietnam will not be won by bullets and bombs. The big job is to make these people believe in us and in themselves.

That's the job of the Green Berets. These Special Forces are dropped from low-flying planes into the middle of the jungle. If they're officers they get a chute. They live in teams of twelve out in the villages with their Vietnamese counterparts. They live off the land. They're trained to survive under any conditions. They chew leaves for moisture. They carry a snake in their shirt for food. They spend so much time in the rice paddies their toenails grow two inches a week. And these guys are cool under fire. If one of them steps on a mine, the other one says, "Shhh!"

In addition, Nha Trang is the home base of the brand-new psychological warfare unit, the Fifth Air Commando Squadron. This unit flies specially built, slow-flying planes equipped with tape-playing machines that can broadcast propaganda messages to enemy troops on the ground. These planes fly day and night, broadcasting messages from captured V.C.s urging their comrades to give up fighting and return home. In addition, they drop thousands of leaflets every day. And while it might not sound effective, they told us that some fourteen hundred V.C. had surrendered in a two-month period. Even in war you can't get away from commercials.

Colonel Clyde Angley, an old friend whom we had met in Labrador four years ago, is in charge of the project. He asked us if we'd like to tape a Christmas message to be broadcast to the Special Forces outposts in the boondocks. Naturally, we were thrilled to do it. I don't remember exactly what I said, but don't be surprised if you see Ho Chi Minh driving a Chrysler.

Backstage, a young medic issued us additional malaria pills. He looked as if he was going to burst into tears at any moment. We found out why. He and his buddy were due to be rotated back to the States in ten days. But last night they found his buddy dead. The Cong had cut off his head, slit open his belly, and stuffed his head into it. Their usual treatment for any GI found carrying dum-dum bullets. They're the bullets that make a one-inch hole going in and a twelve-inch hole coming out.

We had a great house that afternoon. About eight thousand, including Green Berets, Air Force, and all the ambulatory patients from the base hospital. While Les Brown and his Washtub Thumpers were out on stage decimating "Leapfrog," I was in the dressing room tent with our makeup man, Mike Moschella, who generously forsook the girls to assist me in my losing battle against the ravages of time. Just then a kid with a nine-foot southern accent stuck his head in the tent flap and yelled, "Hey, Mistuh Hope, when you all get home tell 'em we're finally fightin' for the right side . . . the South!" It was a great joke and I bought it from him right then, on the spot . . . with a Confederate dollar.

This year we played the show in an open field about a hundred yards from a warehouse full of beer that the Cong had blown up forty-eight hours before. The fools . . . haven't they heard about the "pull-tab tops"?

The year before we played in the middle of the compound, surrounded by buildings and pillboxes with guards patrolling the roofs above us. And just as we neared the end of the show, Colonel Spears walked out and said, "Bob, I would like to present you and your troupe . . . you warriors from Hollywood, with this Viet Cong machine gun." To say the least, I was startled. To say the truth, the damn thing scared me. I said, "That's wonderful, Colonel, just wonderful. Say, would you mind pointing that thing down? I can't see where your other hand is." Fear is really great when it comes to comedy . . . especially when the audience knows you're not kidding. I had to laugh when we got home and saw the film, but I was really pretty jumpy on that stage.

And then another officer, a captain, stepped up to the microphone. It was completely ad lib and unprogrammed, but more than that, I was thrown by his name tag. It said, "Cooley." And that was the name of one of my very closest friends, Charley Cooley, who got me my first job back in the old days when I was sweating it out trying to get started in Chicago. He traveled with me until he died a few years ago. When I saw the name "Cooley," I couldn't quite place it. Was this a relative, or what? Actually, it was mere coincidence. The man's name was Chaplain Cooley, and he asked if he might lead us in prayer.

It was just about sunset, and we bowed our heads. It was suddenly all very quiet. It was a lovely prayer, simply spoken, and thanking God for our nation, our heritage, and asking help and guidance and the strength to carry on our mission.

Just as he finished speaking there was a pause, and then three jets roared out of the sky, buzzed us, and roared off into the sun. It was a shockingly dramatic moment . . . either the wildest coincidence in the world, or somebody up in that big stage in the sky has the makings of a great director.

Oh, and I forgot the most important wild coincidence. The cameras were running and there was film in them. And it was one of the most effective elements in our first Vietnam television show.

Backstage after the show I met two young Vietnamese boys I'll never forget. They wore American Airborne uniforms, and they were only fourteen and fifteen years old. Six months before the V.C. had murdered their parents. The boys knew the whereabouts of the V.C. guerrilla unit, and told the 101st Airborne Rangers.

The V.C. unit was ambushed and wiped out. But the word has spread among the Cong, and now there is a price on these kids' heads of five hundred dollars apiece.

A couple of war orphans adopting Anita Bryant. (NBC Photo by Gary Null)

They were brought to the stage, accompanied by Pfc. Joe Tucker, Ranger of the 1st Airborne Battalion; he was their bodyguard that day, and there were always one or two armed guards who never left their sides. Even in the heavily guarded backstage area where only Americans were allowed, this Ranger never left their sides. Outside the dressing room tents a couple of Vietnamese workers attempted to speak to the boys, but they would not acknowledge them, and were obviously frightened and hid their faces. Both smoked cigarettes, and we were told their greatest joy was in being with the American Rangers and drinking beer with the men.

These were not fourteen- and fifteen-year-old boys as we Americans know. They were suspicious of every stranger, and had fear in their eyes. They both were up on the steps leading to the stage, and watched the antics of Joey Heatherton while she did the Watusi with some of the soldiers. Only then, for the first time, did these Vietnamese orphans giggle and laugh like ordinary children.

These boys have been with the Ranger Battalion for six months, with Rangers schooling them on their own, since schools in that area will not take them. Red tape holds up their being sent to another part of the country for their safety.

As we drove from the show back to our quarters, we could see the devastating effect of the monsoons. The streets were washed away in some instances, and others had huge potholes filled with water. When you hit them, there's a loud thud and all you can think of is a land mine.

With the knowledge that we'd be in a resort town, we expected the accommodations to be rather great. Two years ago they put us up in an old French mansion that must have been built the year Chevalier was born. The shower was in the middle of the room right over the "John." I knew the French did some pretty wild things, but this was ridiculous. True, it did save you a little time,

*Sexy, isn't he?* (*NBC Photo*)

but nobody should be in that much of a hurry. This year I stayed in the same place, but what a difference. Now it was the Commanding General's Headquarters, and General Swede Larson had fixed it up to look like we were on the winning side. The mosquitoes were there, but they were wearing mittens. For Nha Trang it was lush.

I thought our place was O.K., but when I saw where they had put the girls, I felt guilty. They were housed in an area off the base called "The Compound." It consisted of a group of shabby, oddly shaped buildings surrounded by barbed wire. A dirt road cut through the middle and there was a guardhouse at the gate with four fully armed guards on duty at all times. Carroll Baker said it reminded her of a P.O.W. camp.

They put two gals in each room, which measured about ten by twelve, and contained two hospital beds, one wooden chair, a ceiling fan, a bare light bulb, and a ratty-looking cloth that passed for a window curtain.

The bathroom had no soap or towels, which really didn't matter because there wasn't any water. But at least they had company . . . the second-largest roaches I have ever seen. And because they're second, they try harder.

If the girls wanted water to drink or brush their teeth, they had to walk outside to the guardhouse and bring it back in a Dixie Cup.

Adjacent to their barracks building was a ten-foot wall. One of the girls asked a guard what was behind the wall. He replied, "The Viet Cong, ma'am."

Despite the lack of large-scale combat operations in Nha Trang, there is considerable infiltration and sneak suicide attacks. Except for Saigon, this was probably the tightest security we encountered on the entire trip.

In addition to U.S. troops, the base is guarded by Chinese mercenaries called Nungs. The Special Forces guys were very high on these men, informing us that the Nungs would die before they'd leave their post.

Two days before we arrived, a V.C. suicide squad had managed to infiltrate the base and blow up a barracks building just four blocks from the show site.

To prevent this sort of thing, they are now using American guard dogs. These dogs, through their keen sense of smell, can detect the presence of the V.C. long before any electronic device or human being. In turn, the Cong has great respect for these dogs and will not attempt to penetrate an area where these dogs are known to be.

In order to facilitate the handling of sixty-three people and their luggage, our troupe is divided into four groups: The musicians, the technicians, the production staff, and the stars. I'm in the latter category.

Each group has their own color-coded baggage tags, which automatically tells the handlers where to send the luggage. Because we move so fast and so often, there are usually a few bags missing. This is about the only thing that really bugs our tribe. They don't mind getting shot at, but don't fool with their luggage. After a hot, muggy plane ride, it's the worst feeling in the world not to be able to shave, shower, and climb into some clean clothes.

Many of our gang have been traveling together for so long that as soon as their bag is missing they know exactly the right size person to borrow from.

Carroll Baker lost three bags, and Les Helena, our cameraman, lost one. We were really worried about finding Les' bag, because he's nothing without his clothes. Of course, these were just minor incidents. I'll never forget the trip to Alaska, when Jayne Mansfield lost her bra. Now that is a catastrophe. Our entire troupe was declared a disaster area. We applied for Federal aid, under the Wildlife and Conservation Program.

In addition to luggage, we traditionally lose or burn out the hair dryers. This might not sound very drastic to you, but try traveling around the world with five girls and no hair dryer . . . and see if you make it back alive.

*Fred and Ginger?* (*NBC Photo*)

What breaks me up is that they always call me like it was my fault and I should know where to find it. I have enough trouble keeping track of my chin strap.

We were now in our ninth day of the trip, and the heat and the pace was starting to take its toll. Practically everybody had stomach trouble. We had more rumbles than *West Side Story.*

The medics has us on "no-go" pills, but it was a losing battle. At the Officers' Club in Nha Trang, you had to take a number to get into the men's room.

If we wanted to leave the compound we had to call Transportation and a Jeep with armed guards would pick us up and take us where we wanted to go. I had heard through Barney and John Bubbles that there was a great tailor shop downtown, where they were practically giving away magnificent suits . . . sort of a fortune-cookie Hart, Schaffner & Marx. The suits were custom tailored in every detail. Not only was each stitch hand-sewn to every individual wrinkle of your body, but they assigned individual silkworms who labored just for you. The place was called, "The Hongkong Ambassador Tailors in Downtown Nha Trang." And the boss, of course, was a fantastic character named Vic, who was, what else, an Indian.

When I walked into the store I thought Vic must be some kind of a camera nut. I said, "Hello," he flashed a camera in my face. I looked at a suit—FLASH! I picked up a shirt—FLASH! From the time I walked in until the time I left it was like being in the middle of an electrical storm. The merchants are very crafty in this part of the country. They serve beer to the customers. As the customer's oiled, the wallet is greased. Of course, Vic, being an Indian, wasn't too hip with the firewater . . . and he drank more than I did. By the time it came to the haggling he was just no match for me. I had him right where he wanted me.

This last year when I went back to visit Vic, I found out what all the flashbulbs were about. There were full-size blowups of me in the window and all round the store, with signs saying, "Bob Hope's Personal Tailor."

When I left the store, I found a GI in regular clothes, standing on the sidewalk with a submachine gun, actually daring anyone to enter. I said to the GI, "How come you're in civvies?"

He stood there on the main thoroughfare of the town with that big gun under his arm and said, "I didn't want to be conspicuous."

Oh, yes . . . about the suit. It was beautiful. Material? Couldn't have been better. Worksmanship? The finest. And the fit? It fit Dolores absolutely perfectly.

# CHAPTER TEN

Right about here it might be interesting to give you a minute-by-minute account of a day on this tour. As you will see, there are all sorts of problems involved in putting on our type of show ten thousand miles away from home. There are mechanical problems, logistical problems, and human problems which make every day unpredictable and a sort of adventure. Each day has its frustrations, its unforeseen drama, its defeats and victories. So here's one typical day in Vietnam.

*Nha Trang, Wednesday, December 29*

7 A.M.: Clay Daniel, our Assistant Director and unofficial "den mother," who has the responsibility of getting the baggage and personnel ready to leave on schedule, is worriedly pacing in front of our billet, glancing at his watch every few seconds. He rushes into the two-story ramshackle building, pounds on several doors, and yells, "Come on, you guys! Get the lead out! You've got five minutes! Or would you rather we left you here for the Cong?"

From behind a closed door come a few colorful rejoinders. "Whyncha get back on your U-boat?" "We'll be right there, fink!"

Fortunately, Clay has developed an immunity to these barbs. He has reconciled himself to the fact that he's not going to win any popularity contests on these trips. As Clay puts it: "Somebody has to do it. I don't think Job

*"And then Goldilocks said to the three bears . . ."* (*NBC Photo by Gary Null*)

could make this trip as Assistant Director and come back with friends. At the end of each trip, I'm about as popular as King Faisal at a B'nai B'rith dinner."

7:30 A.M.: Breakfast in the mess hall.

Like An Khe, the big topic of discussion is the mosquitoes that plagued everyone during the night. There is an especially virulent type of mosquito in Nha Trang which has hospitalized hundreds of our men and for which our medics have not yet found a cure. One guy comments: "I'm from New Jersey and I've seen mosquitoes, but never monsters like these. Last night, there was one mosquito in my room that was so big, he wrestled the flit-gun right out of my hand and sprayed *me* with it!"

We eat a typical GI breakfast in Vietnam, scrambled eggs, bacon, toast, coffee, and anti-malaria pills.

I notice that Kaye Stevens is sitting off by herself, just staring at her food, and looking pale. Somewhere along the line, she's picked up a bug and has had rough going. I go over and try to cheer her up. I say, "Feeling better?" She says, "Much better, Bob. If I keep improving, by tomorrow I should be strong enough to go on sick call."

She looks weak, but I know that comes show time, Kaye will go on and give a great performance with all the gusto and energy that's characteristic of her.

It's a remarkable thing and hard to explain, but I know from personal experience that doing these shows overseas works a kind of magic. You may be wracked with a cold, running a temperature, be half-cooked with sunburn, or exhausted to the point of collapse, yet when you get on that stage and face that audience, all your ills seem to vanish. The only thing on your mind is that audience and giving them the best performance that's in you. I call it therapy. At least it works that way for me and it seems to apply to everyone else in the cast.

The excitement of it all gets your adrenalin glands pumping. It proves something I've always maintained . . . we get a lot more from those guys than we give them.

9 A.M.: We board the C-130 for the flight to Chu Lai, about two hundred miles away. We get as comfortable as we can in the improvised bucket seats and wait for the takeoff. It's hot in the plane, but we know it'll be cooler when we're airborne. Twenty minutes go by and we're still waiting. Everyone gets fidgety. They look at me accusingly, as though I'm responsible for the delay. I shrug my shoulders as if to say, "Don't stare at me. Write the Pentagon." Another twenty minutes pass. Finally the door at the back of the plane closes, there's a whine, and then

the engines start up with a welcome roar. All but one. The number three engine refuses to cooperate. Now all the engines suddenly die out. The flight engineer appears and tells us we can't use this plane, one of the engines has burned out.

Disgusted, everyone troops off the plane. Fortunately, there is a "backup" plane standing by. We get aboard and this time we're luckier. In a few minutes, we're airborne and headed for Chu Lai.

Despite the grumbling over the inconvenience, I realize how fortunate we were that it happened while we were still on the ground. It's a bit nerve-racking to find out a motor's burned out at twenty thousand feet. It reminded me of an incident that happened during our Christmas tour in 1958, in Vicenza, Italy. In refueling our plane for the flight to Frankfurt, Germany, someone had inadvertently pumped the wrong kind of gas into the tanks. It was the type used by jet fighters stationed at the base and would have exploded in midair had we taken off. Only our pilot's acute sense of smell saved us. He detected the difference just as we were about to climb aboard.

I recall the pilot saying to me, "Bob, with your nose, I'm surprised you didn't smell it first." I had a topper but I was much too grateful to him to use it.

11:15 A.M.: We're over Chu Lai and ready to land. The runway at Chu Lai is short, so we have to make one of those heart-in-your-mouth vertical landings. We get off the plane and take our first look at Chu Lai.

All around is a vast expanse of sand, scrubby pine trees, and just beyond the ocean.

Chu Lai is one of the newer and most active bases in Vietnam, and houses over twenty thousand troops, mostly Marines. The Cong realize its importance and have kept it under almost constant attack. They sneak down from the jungle-covered mountains only a few miles away, launching grenade and mortar attacks from close range.

We were also warned to stick close to the base because the perimeter is heavily mined. It was at Chu Lai that Dickey Chapelle, the famous woman correspondent, was killed when she tripped a mine.

We are greeted by Brigadier General Jonas A. Platt, Base Commander and Assistant Division Commander of the 3rd Marine Division. It was kind of a reunion for us. I'd met General Platt in Plevuva in the South Pacific during World War II just prior to the Marines' invasion of Palau, during which the Leathernecks sustained casualties of 60 per cent.

11:30 A.M.: We are taken to our dressing rooms near the show site. They have given us the use of the chapel to change and make up. It was a simple wooden structure built by the guys with whatever materials they could find. It didn't look like much but to them it looked like a great cathedral.

The show site is located in a natural amphitheater, with the Cong-infested mountains as a backdrop. The stage is made up of four flat-bed trailers covered with plywood. I'm amazed to see an audience of over seven thousand already seated and waiting. I'm told that the fellows have been coming out to the show site each morning for days, as early at 6 A.M., and scrambling for "good seats" up front because they didn't know which day we were coming.

I look up and am flabbergasted. There, high in the trees, are Marines hanging precariously by their cartridge belts, in order to get a better view of the stage.

(In February 1966, Anita Bryant visited the Great Lakes Naval Hospital and came upon a young Marine who was so heavily bandaged, she was afraid to ask him what had happened to him. She found out that during one of her numbers at our show in Chu Lai, his cartridge belt broke and he'd fallen out of the tree.)

11:35 A.M.: I ask an MP to direct me to the men's room. He points to a spot about fifty yards from the show site,

*Write your own caption—and it's a lie. (NBC Photo by Gary Null)*

where a reed canvas-enclosed cubicle sits in the scrub-covered sand. I trudge over and go in. I do a double-take. There on the lid of the "convenience" (as the British call them) is scrawled: "Welcome Bob Hope!" How's that for fame? I've been in many a headline but this is the first time I've had a line in a head! I may yet turn out to be the "Kilroy" of Vietnam.

Sanitary facilities have often been a problem on these tours, especially for the gals. After all, we travel through war zones where privacy is unimportant and usually non-existent.

Although every effort is made to provide the gals with reasonably adequate and clean facilities, the results are frequently a little primitive. Also, the engineers are so anxious to give the girls a modicum of privacy that they locate the "Chic Sales" as far away from the troops as possible. This, though well-intentioned, defeats its purpose since it makes the johns all the more conspicuous.

This situation created one of the most embarrassing moments of our 1964 tour. The scene was the Bayonet Bowl in Seoul, Korea. One of the glamorous stars in the troupe was waiting backstage for her cue to go on, when she got the call. She was wearing a red-spangled costume which could be seen all the way back in Tokyo. The GIs had thoughtfully located the powder room about a quarter of a mile away from the stage, in a little hut standing all by itself about as unnoticeable as a soda fountain in the middle of the Sahara.

Our heroine had no choice. It was now or never. She started to walk, with all the nonchalance she could muster, toward the powder room, which to her seemed at least fifteen miles away. But unfortunately, a gorgeous blonde with a beautiful figure wrapped in a skin-tight flaming red gown, walking through a sea of panting GIs, is apt to be noticed.

She hadn't gone more than twenty-five yards when a roar

went up from the GIs as they became aware of her destination. Wolf whistles filled the air along with shouts of, "Hey, where are you going?" And, "Hope you get a good seat!"

Undaunted, she pressed on, looking neither left nor right, her eyes fixed on her goal, which now seemed farther away than ever. Her face now matched the color of her dress.

After what must have seemed like the longest ordeal since Napoleon's retreat from Moscow, she arrived at "the place" and ducked in quickly.

The "audience" fell silent, but every head was turned in the direction of the little hut.

A few minutes later, she emerged to the greatest spontaneous ovation she had ever received. But this gal won everybody's heart with her response. She bowed deeply from the waist, and ran back to the stage. I must tell you, it was a helluva tough act to follow.

The GIs get a big kick out of seeing their stars and take great pride in being able to do something for them. I still remember a GI on Green Island in the Pacific during World War II who was an ardent fan of Frances Langford. When the guys there got word that we were coming, this fellow showed his affection for Frances in a most unusual way. When I got off the plane, he rushed over to me with a triumphant smile on his face, stuck out a calloused paw, and said, "Shake the hand that dug the can for fabulous Frances Langford!"

In Danang, the guys really outdid themselves in the matter of the girls' personal comfort. Though the best they could come up with in the way of a powder room was rather simple, they compensated for that in a most resourceful way. They piped music into the cubicle. How about that? It must be quite a thrill to be in the middle of a combat zone and wash your hands to the beautiful strains of Tchaikovsky's "Romeo and Juliet Overture."

11:40 A.M.: In the part of the chapel being used for makeup, there is a slight altercation. There is an unwritten rule that those girls who are to be filmed during the show are to be made up first by our greasepaint wizard, Mike Moschella. This is absolutely essential on these trips when facilities are so limited and our schedule is so tight. Now, one of the girls who is not filming has planted herself in the makeup chair and refuses to budge. The girl who is filming can't get her to move. Mike, who is a six-footer and looks more like a football tackle than a makeup man, would like to strangle her. But he realizes that it's been an exhausting tour and nerves are a bit frayed, so he tries to reason with her. But she's adamant. Pressed for time, Mike solves the problem by yanking the chair out from under her.

Mike is one of the unsung heroes of this tour. He not only has the formidable job of making up five sometimes temperamental girls, and me, he must also wrestle with the problems created by the heat and merciless sun of Southeast Asia. To do a really good makeup job that'll last more than three or four minutes under such conditions calls for every bit of ingenuity he can muster.

But I'll let Mike tell you what he was up against: "I start with grease, and really spread it on. But the girl is perspiring so much, it runs right off her face, and I have to go to pancake. Now I find my eyebrow pencils and lipsticks have melted right in the case, so I have to dip them in ice water, if I can get some. I ask one of the guys if he can possibly find me a couple of ice cubes, a rare item in Vietnam. A girl goes on and does her number and by the time she comes back, every bit of makeup has disappeared and I've got to start from scratch.

Another thing I have to contend with is sunburn. The sun goes completely through the makeup and their noses and foreheads start to peel and their arms get all blotchy and red. By the time the tour is over, they all look like leopards."

Of course, Mike didn't have any problems with my

209

makeup. He's been making me up for so long, he knows every nook, ridge, and cranny in my face. He just takes a pound of putty and a spatula and within five minutes, I look like a reject from Mount Rushmore.

11:43 A.M.: A pleasant note. Joey Heatherton is having a reunion with a former high school classmate and boy friend, Marine Lieutenant Michael Harrigan, from Rockville Centre, Long Island, who's stationed at Chu Lai. General Westmoreland has arranged for Mike to be off duty during Joey's stay and also to accompany her to our next stop, Danang. Talk about the luck of the Irish!

11:45 A.M.: At the show site, Alan Stensvold is making a last-minute check of the cameras that have been mounted on platforms by his crew. They've been at Chu Lai for over two hours, doing all the strenuous work involved in setting up the heavy mobile platforms and cameras.

Alan and his men are complete professionals who volunteer enthusiastically for these trips year after year. Some of them take time out from comfortable studio jobs to go on these rough tours. Others maintain membership in the cameramen's union and pay their dues just so they can work our Christmas shows. Felber Maasdam, for instance, does very well in his own manufacturing business, and Les Helena is a successful producer of educational films. Yet for about two weeks every year, they leave their families, their businesses, and the comforts of home and put up with the hardships and privations of our annual treks.

It's quite a tribute to us, especially in view of the fact that many of these guys are no longer kids. Bert Eason, for instance, is nudging seventy, yet he's the first to volunteer before he even knows where we'll be heading. The average age of our camera crew is about sixty, yet they do a magnificent job under adverse conditions with the pep and vitality of vitamin-filled teen-agers. It's a great testimonial to prune juice.

Another man I've been lucky enough to have on these

*Volunteers?* (*NBC Photo*)

trips since 1954 is Colonel Woody Mark. The Air Force assigns Woody to us to expedite the moving of the equipment from base to base. As a longtime motion picture cameraman, he also pinch-hits with the "IMO," the hand-held camera which, because of its mobility, is invaluable in getting shots beyond the range of the fixed cameras.

There's quite a story in Woody. In 1943, while working at Universal Studios, he was sworn into the Air Force by Ronald Reagan, who was then the adjutant of the first motion picture unit. His Commanding Officer was Paul Mantz, the greatest stunt flyer in movie history, who was killed recently during the filming of *The Flight of the Phoenix*.

Woody was assigned as a combat cameraman to the Fifteenth Air Force in Italy and soon after was sent on his first mission, a dangerous bombing run over the strategic Ploesti oil fields in Rumania. He barely had time to aim his camera when his B-29 was hit by flak over the target. He and the ten other members of the crew were forced to bail out. For Woody, it was his first parachute jump. But I'll let him tell it: "In those days there were no schools to teach you how to jump or when to pull the cord. So we all just got out the best way we could, and pulled the ripcord whenever we felt like it, which in my case was right away.

"So there we were, eleven of us, floating down from twenty thousand feet, with heavy flak coming up at us, and the bombs from our own planes dropping down. I had the craziest thought that I'd seen it all before in a dozen war movies, and here it was actually happening to me.

"I was never so scared in my life. I didn't think we'd ever get down alive, but all of a sudden the ground came up and hit me. We landed in a cornfield with Germans all around us. By some fluke, none of us was injured. They took us to Ploesti, which is about fifty miles from Bucharest, and threw us into an old high school in the center of town. It was enclosed by barbed wire, and was right across the street from some beautiful cafes. Then every night for six months we listened to wild Rumanian music and dancing and the gay laughter of beautiful women. It was really frustrating. We felt like vegetarians at an LBJ barbecue. We were finally liberated by the Russians, and two days later we were picked up by our own planes and flown back to our base in Italy.

"From then on, I was known as "Half-mission Mark.""

11:47 A.M.: I'm in the dressing room checking the monologue when Sil Caranchini comes in and says: "We're running a little late, Bob." I say, "What do you mean?" He says, "'Hanoi Hannah' just announced that the show started at eleven-thirty." I say, "Really? How did I do?"

"Hanoi Hannah" is very popular with the Marines at Chu Lai because she's one of the very few diversions they have. There are no nightclubs, bars, or much of anything else in the way of recreation in the area. The nearest liberty town is Danang, and as one Marine put it: "That's like being allowed to leave the state prison to go to the county jail."

11:50 A.M.: A perspiring Johnny Pawlek has just finished checking the twenty-four loudspeakers around the show site. These speakers have been very hard to come by. They were begged, borrowed, and stolen from bases all over Vietnam. This is one type of equipment that has to be provided by the base in order for us to be able to do a show there. We couldn't possibly carry this much heavy gear with us, nor do we have the three or four days it takes to set them up.

Johnny is smiling, which means everything in the sound department has been done to satisfy his exacting standards. He walks into my dressing room sipping a bottle of local beer called "Bière La Rue" which the Marines have nicknamed "Tiger Beer."

He says, "Boy, this is powerful stuff. You've gotta blow the head off before it blows *your* head off!"

12 noon: I'm waiting back of the stage for the show to start. A few feet away is a chain link fence behind which a group of young Marines are watching the backstage activi-

ties with great fascination. Evidently the two-shows-a-day schedule is beginning to show. One kid shouts through the fence, "Hey, Mr. Hope, you look tired. Why don't you *send* for the troops next Christmas?"

This breaks me up and gives me a much-needed lift.

12:05 P.M.: Les Brown and the boys strike up "Leapfrog" and the show is on. This has been Les' opening number on our Christmas shows for a lot of years. I've heard it all around the world under all sorts of conditions . . . in the frozen wastes of Thule, Greenland, in the scorching sands of Wheelus Air Force Base in Tripoli, in Turkey, Guantánamo, Port Lyautey, Morocco, Tokyo, Naples, Berlin . . . and it never fails to have an electric effect on me. It has a zing and a drive that brings the whole place to life. There's something about hearing that swinging music way out in the jungle that gets you. The guys can't believe that a great band like Les' has come all the way out to their remote spot just to play for them.

Les and the band really play up a storm. Which is great for me. By the time I walk out to do my monologue, everyone is charged up already.

12:10 P.M.: Les goes into "Thanks for the Memory" and I stride on stage and walk confidently to the mike. I look out over the heads of the audience and my confidence vanishes.

Barney McNulty, who should be poised and ready to turn the idiot cards on which my monologue is printed, is nonchalantly taking pictures of the audience and the surrounding area with his ever-present Leica. I'm ready, but Barney isn't!

Barney's a man of many interests. He's a student of native customs, art connoisseur, bargain hunter, gourmet, and one of the world's most rabid photographers. In fact, he takes more pictures on our tours than NBC.

I sometimes think Barney considers me a great inconvenience.

I can't just stand there, so I say, "It's wonderful to be here in Chu Lai," hoping somebody will get Barney's attention back to the cards. Our director, Mort Lachman, yells, "Let's go, Barney! You can finish the *Life* layout later!"

Barney responds quickly. He swings around to the cards which are strapped loosely to a ladder which is serving as a makeshift rack. A little too quickly. His arm hits the ladder, sending the cards cascading to the ground.

Brilliant ad libber that I am, I yell, "Stop the war! My idiot cards are gone!"

I'm in a mild panic, but Barney hasn't lost his cool. He clambers down from his perch and starts retrieving the cards and putting them in their proper order. In the middle of this, he looks up at me and yells, "This may take a few minutes, Bob. Why don't you do a few choruses of 'Buttons and Bows'?"

That's what I like about Barney. He makes up for an inexcusable goof with an unforgivable line.

12:15 P.M.: I launch into my monologue. It's been tailored for the Marines:

"I'm thrilled to be here in John Wayne-land.

"Sorry we're a little late. We had one of those chicken pilots who won't fly just because there's a couple of motors missing.

"But I'm happy to be here with the Marines. Their motto is 'Semper Fidelis,' which means, 'Let's call a twenty-four-hour truce and sort teeth.

"The other bases invited me. This one *dared* me!

"You know how they say a Marine is so tough, he can eat nails. . . . I ate one at the Marine mess hall last night and it was the best thing on the menu.

"Yes sir, this is the most secret base I've ever visited. Everything is strictly hush-hush. At dawn, the bugler just *thinks* reveille. Then he tiptoes from bunk to bunk and whispers, 'The General's up. . . . How about you?'"

215

And so on. The monologue runs about twelve minutes and is well received by not only the Marines but also by the Seabees, Combat Engineers, Special Forces troops, medics, airmen, and a sprinkling of hospital patients in the audience.

12:30 P.M.: I introduce Joey Heatherton, who's on next. She doesn't appear. I look toward the wings. Clay Daniels, with frantic hand and arm signals, indicates that Joey's not ready and points to Kaye Stevens, who's standing next to him. I get the message and introduce Kaye.

12:32 P.M.: I go back to the improvised dressing room in the chapel to find out what's happening with Joey. I discover her in the midst of a group of Marines, one of whom is yanking on the zipper of her white dancing boot. It's gotten stuck halfway which is why she couldn't go on and do her Watusi number. Joey's very apologetic and on the verge of tears. I tell her it's O.K. and add, "If these Marines can't get the zipper fixed, we'll call in the Combat Engineers."

1:10 P.M.: Back on stage. Les and the boys go into "You Are Too Beautiful," and I bring on Carroll Baker. The applause, yells, and whistles are so earthshaking they probably register on the seismograph at Cal Tech.

Carroll and I go into what we call an "intimate" spot in which we throw lines at each other, with her getting the best of it. Here are a few excerpts that the guys seemed to really appreciate:

HOPE: (*indicating audience*) How do you like this group of tigers, huh?

CARROLL: Oh, they make a beautiful sight. It looks like one big dessert tray.

HOPE: Yeah—that's been left out in the sun too long. Carroll, you're considered the sexiest gal in movies today, isn't that so?

CARROLL: Bob, my pictures aren't meant to be that sexy. It's all in the mind.

Hope: It *is*, huh? (*to audience*) You're all under arrest! (*to Carroll*) I loved you in *Harlow*. I've never seen such sexy and revealing gowns.

Carroll: I was a little hoarse when I made that movie, didn't you notice?

Hope: I didn't even know it was a talkie!

Carroll: Bob, how is it we've never been in a picture together?

Hope: Oh, I think the Code only allows one sex symbol at a time.

Carroll loved doing this routine with me. She'd been playing screen *femmes fatales* for so long, when she brought out the garbage, the women in the neighborhood would hide their husbands. So when she got this chance to do some comedy, she reveled in it, and proved surprisingly adept at getting laughs.

1:32 P.M.: Al Borden, our prop man, is setting up the stage for the medical sketch. In the dressing room, another crisis is in the making. Kaye Stevens, who plays the nurse, has put on her cape and complains that it's too heavy to wear in the oppressive heat. To make it more comfortable, she starts to rip out the lining.

Charlie Solomon, the warden of the wardrobe, spots her and is outraged. He rushes over, grabs the cape out of her hand, and says, "You can't rip this cape. It's gotta go back to Western Costume." Kaye says, "I should have known. It feels like it belongs on a horse."

Charlie, however, convinces her to wear the cape, lining and all, because it's an authentic World War II nurse's cape and that Mr. Hope insists on authenticity in even the smallest detail. His name isn't Solomon for nothing.

Charlie is another veteran of these tours—he's made about a dozen of them and has learned diplomacy the hard way. On one trip, he handled the costumes for Zsa Zsa Gabor. He's been invaluable to me as personal dresser on all my TV comedy specials. Some of our sketches call for out-

*Carroll Baker—monogramming my parachute under the watchful eye of Charlie Solomon, our shop steward. (NBC Photo by Gary Null)*

landish outfits. But nothing throws Charlie. He somehow comes up with any kind of costume, no matter how bizarre, that the writers dream up . . . and they think up some lulus. One that comes to mind was in a "Batgirl" sketch we did with Martha Raye in which I played a villain who was "Half man, half lobster." The costume was so realistic the stage crew tried to stuff me with crabmeat. And once he provided me with a hillbilly outfit that was so convincing, after the show I rushed home and built a still in the basement.

Charlie's become my "caloric conscience." I have a sweet tooth for pastries of all kinds, but the mere thought of Charlie's disapproval has often stayed my fork on its way to a gorgeous slab of banana cream pie. Charlie doesn't know it, but he's cost Sara Lee a fortune.

1:45 P.M.: Joey Heatherton, the zipper fixed, is singing "Gimme a Little Kiss" to six thousand or so bug-eyed Marines who look only too anxious to oblige. From this she goes into her wild Watusi dance with a frenzied abandon which brings the audience to its feet. Swaying, kicking, and leaping with tigerlike grace, to the pulsating rhythm of the bongos, she creates a riotous excitement that infects the Marines and drives many of them into the aisles where they dance along with her.

Now Les Brown invites half a dozen guys to come up on stage and Watusi with Joey. It has the same effect as dangling a transfer back to the States in front of them. A stampede ensues. The MPs stem the tide and allow about six Marines up on stage, who form a circle around Joey and go into the wildest dance this side of Tanganyika. It's quite a sight to see these rugged bruisers with their heavy combat boots shaking, squirming, and gyrating with the airy dexterity of a Nureyev. The crowd loves it. We've done a lot of frantic audience participation bits, but for sheer hysteria this tops them all.

2 P.M.: The show ends with a number in which the five

girls complain in song about the trials and tribulations they've endured on this tour with me, how I tricked them into going overseas, my hamminess, the despotic manner in which I run the show, and a host of other beefs. It's all tongue-in-cheek . . . I *think*.

There are big yaks all through this musical colloquy, but it ends on a serious but hopeful note with the entire cast singing, to the tune of "Together":

"And though we really love to roam
We hope next year we'll all be back home
Together
In peace and goodwill."

2:20 P.M.: The audience is dispersing. The crew is dismantling the camera platforms, and packing up the electrical equipment and other gear so it can be loaded onto trucks and taken to the plane. We're due in Danang at three-thirty and we're running behind.

Just before we left for the runway, one of the Marines asked me, "Is it true John Wayne is coming out next?"

"That's the scuttlebutt," I said.

And Duke did go. I talked to him about the trip when he got back. This is what he had to say:

"The only guys who are complaining about the war are back here. From what I saw in Vietnam, from an aircraft carrier in the China Sea to the bunkers in the Plain of Reeds, everyone in this country should be mighty thankful to the finest bunch of men any nation ever put into action.

"As far as I am concerned, every one of them is starspangled American."

2:55 P.M.: We've said good-bye to General Platt, signed our last autograph, and are back in our C-130 waiting for the takeoff. This time there's no hitch. The takeoff is smooth and we're soon airborne and headed for Danang and another date with the Marines.

# CHAPTER ELEVEN

En route to Danang I had a quick meeting with Colonel Larry Glaab. Three days earlier, Colonel Bob Gates told me that his Commander in the Philippines urgently requested that if at all possible they would like the Bob Hope troupe to visit the hospital at Clark Field.

Our schedule had been very tightly worked out by the Defense Department. Transportation was also a big problem. But I told Bob that we would certainly do the show if the military could figure out a way to work it.

Larry Glaab jumped on it right then and there, and had been on the horn ever since, trying to work it out. He now told me that Major General Wilson of Clark Field had managed to get two T-39s, small twin-engine jets, that could whip us across the South China Sea to the Philippines in a hurry.

Eight of us could leave immediately after the show, whip over to Clark, and do the hospital. Meanwhile, the rest of the cast and crew would break camp, pack, have dinner, and pick us up at Clark Field in the Big Bird. Not an hour would be lost, and we would make the show in Guam on time.

Larry said, "Bob, I know it's tight, and not the most pleasant trip in the world in those small jets, but they really want the show at Clark."

I said, "Larry, don't spin your oak leaves. I've talked to the gals and Jerry and they all want to do it, and I've

221

*After each show I leave quickly under an assumed name. (NBC Photo by Gary Null)*

drafted Bobby Gibbons for guitar and we're all set. Just have those jets smoking when we finish the show in Danang."

The city of Danang, or "Dogpatch," as it is called by the GIs, is said to be the home of some ten thousand Viet Cong. It is also the site of our northernmost airbase in Vietnam and the scene of more plots, revolts, strikes, riots, and demonstrations than the campus at Berkeley.

It was a hot, muggy, dank-gray afternoon, and as we stepped off the plane, our suntans were bathed in a torrent of rain. In a matter of seconds we were soaked to the skin, our clothes plastered against us. It was no place for a girl with anything to hide.

We were met by my good friend, Marine Commander Major General Lewis W. Walt, who had first welcomed our troupe twenty-two years before on Pavuvu in the South Pacific, when he was with the 1st Marines.

Walt, who was promoted to major general in May of '65, was promoted again to three-star general a few weeks after our visit in Danang, for the tremendous job being done by his 3rd Marine Amphibious Force.

He's not only a great soldier, but a big booster for entertainers. He really put it on for our outfit, and he was a big factor in arranging for Martha Raye's four-month tour. He's crazy about Martha, and, needless to say, Martha is crazy about him. In fact, she's proposed to him two hundred times.

The rain was really streaming when the General grabbed me by the arm and led me over to his helicopter. He was wearing a poncho and had on combat boots. I was wearing a skinny sports shirt, hazel golf slacks, and green loafers.

We made quite a sight. The General marching through the mud like he was advancing on the enemy, and me trying to tippy-toe my way around the puddles to keep the rain out of my loafers. It was a losing battle. By the time we got to the 'copter my Dr. Scholl's footpads had gone down for the third time.

As we flew from the base to his quarters, we passed right over five thousand GIs sitting in the rain waiting for the show. He told me that some of them had been sitting there since eight that morning, when our show was first announced. It was hard to believe. I know *I* certainly would sit in the rain to see me, but I suppose some of them were waiting for the girls.

The General's headquarters were high up on a mountain that had been captured from the V.C. On a clear day I imagine you could see forever, but even in the sporadic rain

*Underneath that frightened exterior is a frightened interior. (NBC Photo by Gary Null)*

you could see for miles. You could see the 'copters taking off, platoons moving out, and on the wall you could see the map which marked the deployment of troops and artillery. There was no line marking the front. As General Walt explained, "It's a war of small units. Every platoon sergeant is a general. The territory taken means nothing." It's a war of "kill counts" . . . theirs and ours. You score it like a baseball game . . . home team versus the visitors.

Here we met several celebrities, one of whom was my great friend, Senator Stuart Symington, who was on tour of military installations in Vietnam. The Senator from Missouri is one of our great Americans. He might have been President, only he was born two states away. He was largely responsible for my making these trips. He started it all when he was Secretary of the Air Force by inviting us to go to Berlin during the airlift in '49. I figured he was in Danang to see if I'd improved any.

General Walt also introduced me to Lieutenant General Nguyen Chanh Thi, who was Supreme Commander of the I Corps Area, or northern part of South Vietnam. He was one of the country's leading generals, and a member of Premier Ky's military junta. Later he was in the center of the Buddhist uprising in Danang and Hue. It was a nasty situation up there, and for several weeks nobody knew who was for what or why. In fact, later we did a joke about what a problem it was to the demonstrators in this country.

"I met one kid who had a blank picket sign, a pencil, and an eraser. I said, 'What are you doing?' And he said, 'Trying to keep up with Huntley and Brinkley.'"

For a while it looked as though Thi would be executed, but then he served a sixty-day sentence—at a villa, and last I heard left Saigon under secret orders and is now in this country visiting his sons.

When we arrive at a base the officers and men are very eager to see the cast. Let's be even more specific . . . they want to see the girls. In the confusion that ensues, the band is usually ignored and left standing on the runway with egg on their embouchures. Danang was no different from any other place. But it was no problem to Butch Stone.

When it comes to promoting transportation for the band, Butch makes Hertz look like a hitchhiker. Seeing that the band was not as renowned as they were led to believe, Butch immediately commandeered a passing truck.

The driver politely explained that he was on a mission and could not possibly stop and help.

In a style that would make Sergeant Bilko cringe, Butch

said, "You hear that? The man's in a hurry! Pile in fast . . . we don't want this cat to be late for his mission."

Once again the driver pleaded, but Butch just smiled and said, "How are you? Glad to see you! Hut-two-three-four! On the double!"

As the men piled into the truck, a colonel rushed up and assured Butch that the instruments would be delivered to the show site immediately. Butch never lets anyone below the rank of colonel handle the horns.

It was a ten-mile ride in the pouring rain over a dirt road that had been washed out about three times a week. The ruts were so deep that at times the truck almost disappeared from sight. On top of this, the tarp that covered the truck leaked in about twelve places.

As they sat there drenched and clinging to the benches to keep from bouncing around, Butch smiled and said, "Beats walking, eh guys?!"

Little Stumpy Brown, who was in midair at the moment, agreed because the mud was deeper than he was.

When the choppers finally delivered us to the show site the mud was about eight inches deep. Everyone took off his shoes and just kind of oozed his way toward the tent dressing rooms.

A burly Marine, wearing a tag with Carroll Baker's name on it, appeared. Carroll asked him what it was all about, and he replied, "I'm your personal bodyguard, ma'am. Every member of the troupe has been assigned a bodyguard. In case of attack just stay with me. I'll direct you to the back of the tent where an armored van is waiting to evacuate you."

The van was an amtrac with armor plating and gun turrets. "Are you anticipating any trouble?" Carroll asked gingerly.

"No, but just the same, don't go any place without me." And with this, he picked her up and carried her through the mud to her dressing room. When they got about halfway there, a major with a pretty fair sense of humor said, "Corporal, I'm relieving you of your command. Hand me that girl!" The corporal looked him right in the eye and said, "Sir, if you plan to take this girl away from me, I suggest you enlist the aid of at least a hundred men."

The major retreated to regroup his forces.

Kaye Stevens was having a time navigating the muck and slime in her boots until a handsome six-foot, four-inch boy scooped her up and carried her across the mud. Kaye said to him, "Kiddo, I weigh 135 pounds. I hope you know what you're doing."

He replied, "Miss Stevens, if I knew what I was doing, I wouldn't be in Vietnam."

That day in Danang made quite an impression an all of us, especially Kaye. She still has the muddy boots she wore that day and refuses to clean them. She says they remind her of a memorable experience that she never wants to forget. I must remember that the next time Dolores tells me I need a shine.

Just before I went on stage a security officer handed me a note from Major John Darby of the 390th Tactical Fighter Squadron, wishing us the best of luck and expressing their regret at not being able to catch the show. They were on standby alert, and in case anything happened they had to be airborne in a matter of seconds. I was sorry that they had to miss the show, but happy to hear they were there.

As Anita Bryant was getting ready for her number, she noticed a young GI mumbling to himself. She asked him what it was all about and he told her that after waiting for the show from 8 A.M. until now (it was 5 P.M.) he had been ordered back to his outpost on the perimeter.

She sent him back to duty with lipstick all over his face. He didn't wait for the chopper . . . he flew himself!

We had eighty-five hundred men in the audience when we got under way. This means that about three thousand were on duty in the hills kicking the Cong around (local expression). We hadn't anticipated the rain or the mud, so a few ad libs were in order:

"Don't just sit there . . . plant rice!

"I've never seen this much mud. You have to wipe your feet before you put your rubbers on.

"I had a great arrival. I stepped off the plane and disappeared."

At this point I was interrupted by a burly MP, and that's what it takes to interrupt my monologue . . . a burly MP. He got between me and the microphone, which isn't easy to do without combat training, to make the following announcement:

"All personnel from Kilo 412 and attachments report to the helipad immediately." This poor kid was greeted with boos like you wouldn't believe. You'd have thought it was Juan Marichal taking a bow in Dodger Stadium.

It was getting dark and they were calling the men back to the hills to man the nighttime defenses. We knew what the guys wanted to see, and so they wouldn't miss dessert we revised the routine. We opened the show with what would usually be our finale—a number with all five gals and the guys.

What a spot poor Jack Jones was in. Here he was in front of eight thousand rain-soaked guys, fresh out of a jungle, and he has to walk out on stage without an introduction. Worse than that, he blocked their view of the goodies. They screamed for him to move back and get out of the way. Man, I wouldn't have given that spot to Mao Tse-tung.

Kaye Stevens was a beaut on stage that day. She had a georgeous beaded gown (twenty-five hundred, at least, and not even drip-dry). It wasn't exactly what the couturier had in mind for that mud hollow, but it was the last show in Vietnam and Kaye couldn't resist. It stopped raining briefly, but when Kaye stepped on stage the gates opened and the rain came pouring down. The lyric to Kaye's song opened with, "Gee, but it's good to be here on a wonderful day like today." The absurdity of the situation hit the guys and they broke up.

Her next line was, "I defy any cloud to appear in the sky." By now the guys were gone.

"I dare any raindrop to plop in my eye." By the time Kaye finished, her mascara was all over her face and her false eyelashes had slipped to the point where she resembled Colonna.

I don't have to tell you the kind of ovation she got. And it was well-deserved. They should have given her a Bronze Star for that day.

The rain continued as I introduced Miss U.S.A., Diana Lynn Batts. I don't know what the fellows see in her. Maybe she reminds them of their mothers. Whatever it is, you sure don't have to ask for a hand. Diana and I did a little talk spot together, and in one of her lines she says that her father is a Marine. You say the word "Marine" in front of an Air Force or Army audience, and you're lucky if you don't get shelled on stage. That's the true meaning of *esprit de corps* . . . it means "Hate all the others." For Diana, this was a big day, a big rainy day, but she was thrilled to be playing a Marine base at last.

As I remember, the dialogue went something like this:

I'd say, "Diana, I'm sure these fellows want to know all about you. Where were you born?"

"I was born in Camp Le Jeune, North Carolina. Dad was a Marine."

I said, "Well, that figures. Those Marines never waste a weekend pass. Diana, what are your measurements?"

"Well, I'm sure the fellows wouldn't be interested in that."

This brought a rather lusty reaction from the audience. And I said, "Well, Diana, why don't you just whisper them to me?" Which she did. And there were groans

*Smiling Stu Symington in Danang. That was before he heard my monologue. (NBC Photo by Gary Null)*

from the audience. And then one poor kid stood up and yelled, "Please, Mr. Hope . . . we have to know . . . it's important!"

I haven't figured out why it was so important, but her measurements were 37-23-37; which are considerably smaller than mine, but got a lot more applause.

By now the rain was really sogging us, and Diana's beautiful hairdo was slowly turning to spaghetti. I saw Les Brown standing in the wings with her coat and I nodded at him to bring it out. I put the coat over her shoulders and you've never heard such hate from an audience. I still haven't got all the shrapnel out of one leg. I put my coat on and they applauded.

It was pitch dark and we were working mostly by flash-light. The dark was a problem for me, but not for Joey Heatherton. With her act she doesn't need idiot cards. She flew around that sloppy plywood stage like she was working the Grand Ballroom of the Waldorf-Astoria. Neither sleet nor snow nor dark of night could stay that Watusi. And I knew then that nothing could stop these five gals from completing their mission.

Before we closed the show I introduced Senator Syming-ton, who read a very warm and congratulatory message to the show troupe from President Johnson. We thanked the Senator, and as he waved good-bye and headed for his 'copter, he disappeared into the sea of mud, looking just a little like Lloyd Bridges.

I tried to get General Walt on stage to close the show, but by now the monsoon was in full force. I tried to say something on the microphone, but you couldn't hear a word over the pounding of the rain on the stage. The guys were all racing for their 'copters and trucks. The band was covering their instruments and swimming for the tents, except for John Worster, who was surfing on his bass fiddle.

I apologized to the General. He said, "Don't worry about it, you've got to get to those T-39s. They're waiting for you at Clark." We joined the swim for the 'copters.

# CHAPTER TWELVE

A T-39 is a small jet trainer. And I mean tiny! It could take off from the washroom of a 707. And, to put it mildly, it's a tight fit for four passengers. Especially when one of them is all achin' and racked with pain.

After the Danang rain I knew it was going to take me at least two weeks just to dry out. I was beat, banged, battered, and bruised. My body hadn't made up its mind whether to have malaria, dysentery, or dengue fever. However, the combination of rain and heat wasn't a total loss. It cured my fungus condition. Well, it didn't exactly cure it, it just rusted away.

More than anything else at the moment I wanted a nice, comfortable blotter to stretch out on. But there's no stretching on a T-39. Mostly there's just holding your breath. What I really needed at that moment was a drink.

I reached for the button to ring for the steward, but there was no steward and there was no button. Just my big, fat thumb pressed against the wall. But somebody read my mind. That beautiful Bob Gates. Before we left he put two Thermos bottles filled with vodka and orange juice on the plane.

I opened the Thermos, took a deep draught, and became a full-fledged Phil Harris disciple. It was instant transfusion. That booze raced through my blood like it was a speedway. I don't know why the Red Cross wastes its time with coffee and doughnuts when orange juice is so exhilarating.

Now I know what they mean by artificial resuscitation. My head cleared, my spine untangled, and my toes uncurled. I opened my eyes and saw something that did me more good than the vodka.

On the second T-39 were Jerry, Bobby Gibbons, Carroll, and Joey. With me were Anita, Kaye, and Diana, and you wouldn't believe these chicks. Diana, adjudged the most beautiful woman in the United States, got on the plane with her hair looking like it won fourth prize in a mushroom grower's derby. That rain had left her with hair that only Phyllis Diller could love.

And there is one of the biggest stars of the business, Anita Bryant, with pins in her mouth and a comb in her hand, putting up Diana's hair. And doing a great job. I asked her how she knew what she was doing and she said, "Don't worry about me, Bob, I'm a pro by birth. My mother used to be a beauty operator."

Now don't get me wrong. These kids are both sugar and spice. They'll fight you with knives and brass knuckles for top billing on a show. Just misspell a name in a poster and they'd cut your heart out with a manicure scissors. They want the prettiest gown on the stage, the best arrangement, and the best choreographer. Show business is not an easy game for a gal, and none of them got to the top by sitting in a corner hiding their talent under a potato sack.

But let a child like Diana get in trouble and the old pros all pitch in. They helped her with her gowns, they helped her with her makeup, they counseled her against men, and here was Anita flying through the night at seven hundred miles an hour, fixing Diana's coiffure. I was so emotionally shook I didn't mind when I didn't get my "next."

When we landed at Clark Field there were three thousand people waiting on the runway with a stage and microphone all set up. Colonel Arthur B. Tarrow, the doctor who bandaged my ankle in Bangkok, had a red carpet leading right from the planes to the stage, just to make sure I didn't injure it again. We did a fast introductory show and then headed for the hospital.

We did a big show in the hospital for all the ambulatory patients, nurses and doctors, and then moved to the ward rooms. About those ward rooms. They contain patients under intensive care, and you need a strong stomach to go in there and see what these kids have been through. But I had a message and a present for one kid, from his buddies in the Marines at Chu Lai, and I was determined to see him.

I was about to enter his ward when a doctor stopped me and said, "I don't know whether you should see him." I said, "I've got to see him." The minute I walked in I knew what he meant. The kid was lying face up, staring at the ceiling, on a round pad that was vibrating. Twenty-four hours a day he had to lie there while the pad kept shaking. It was the only way they could keep his circulation going. It was sad. I had all these things from his buddies, books, pictures, messages, but I couldn't get through to him. He got through to me, though.

In another ward at the same time, Kaye Stevens was having a slightly different experience. As Kaye told it to me later, "I remember taking my bows and then turning to walk away, when I heard this voice say, 'Hey, Merry Christmas, stupid.' And I looked and it was this same kid I had met at the 3rd Field Hospital in Saigon. He was still a mass of tape and splints and casts, but he was smiling. And I said, 'How come you're so cheery now?' And he said, 'I wasn't feeling too good that day in Saigon, but after you left I got to thinking about it, and you were right. I was alive and I am alive today.' And he started laughing, and he said, 'My name's Frenchy.' And I said, 'Hello, Frenchy, how're you doing?' And he said, 'I'm doing just fine, thanks . . . can I have my Christmas kiss now?' So I gave him his Christmas kiss, and we laughed."

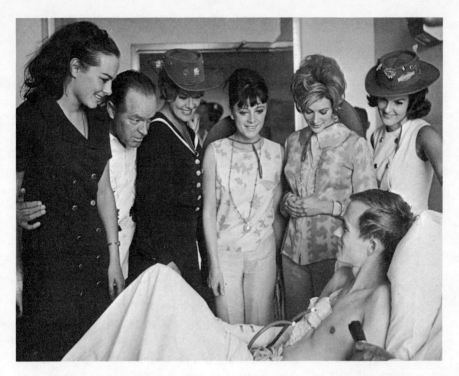

*A patient at Clark AFB hospital pretending he's looking at me. (NBC Photo by Frank Carroll)*

An hour later we did another show, completely unrehearsed. We were the star attraction at dinner in the enlisted men's mess. Ever try to eat with three thousand GIs watching? They applauded every burp. This may open a whole new career for Jackie Gleason.

It was two in the morning when we finally left Clark Air Force Base after our sobering visit. The rest of the cast and crew picked us up in the StarLifter and about two hours out, just after dark, our pilot, Major Kastner, spotted parachute flares some fifteen miles off the port side of our C-141. It was apparent that an air rescue operation was in

235

progress. A Navy jet reconnaissance aircraft had gotten hung up with an uncontrollable engine fire in flight and its four-man crew bailed out. We learned the next day that three of the four crew members had been picked up within a couple of hours of bailing out. A fantastic accomplishment in the middle of the Pacific Ocean at night.

After that we had a wonderful night's rest until seven in the morning when we arrived at our destination—Guam, the world-famous rest area for sharks.

Guam is a very strategic base—really a lifeline for travelers like us—it's our last chance before returning to the States to get tax-free booze. It also has some other strategic value, like being the SAC base for our B-52 raids that have really demoralized the Viet Cong. As recently as 1962 there were still four Japanese holding out on the island, but they finally surrendered. The talk was that there were still two left out there in the hills. Maybe that's why they invited me to entertain. If everything else fails, my act usually smokes 'em out.

We were all so tired, our C-141 didn't exactly touch down, it sort of crept along the runway, but the reception given us by Major General William J. Crumm and his escort of Navy and Air Force officers brought us right back up there. And it's pretty tough to sleep through a Navy band. When the General threw a lei around my neck, it's lucky he didn't kiss me on both cheeks, or I'd have curled up for a nap on his lap. We were told that we had until 3 P.M. to rest and get ready for the show, and the cast was to be driven to their quarters, but on the way there General Crumm told us that about five hundred pilots and crewmen would miss our show because their B-52s were leaving on a mission at eleven twenty-four, and I was very concerned. Somebody was just not syncing up the war with my performances. I quickly rounded up Jerry Colonna and Carroll Baker and asked if they'd volunteer for a performance. Jerry had no problem, but Carroll was already in bed with her makeup off, but when I explained the nature of the emergency, she quickly performed a little *Baby Doll* magic, and we were escorted into the combat briefing room.

And right there she was paid off. That's a moment I'll never forget. The General said "Attention," and five hundred pairs of feet hit the floor absolutely together and five hundred chairs moved back in one sweep, and they were like parts of some wonderful machine as they stood there, barely breathing, as we walked down the aisle. Then the General said, "At ease." And they started to applaud and I hadn't even opened my mouth yet. Maybe they were trying to tell me something. We did an impromptu show for about a half hour. I tried not to be too funny, as I didn't want them to forget their targets. After the performance we went down to the flight line to watch them take off.

As these high-altitude sharpshooters faded into the horizon, I took a few deep breaths, being careful not to overdo it, and we finally got to bed after twenty-four hours of U.S.O. that included Nha Trang, Chu Lai, Danang, Clark Field, and Guam—the most exciting twenty-four hours anyone could spend.

At 3 P.M. there were twenty thousand of our military personnel overflowing Gilkeson Field, and they were ready to be entertained. Some of them had pitched tents the night before and slept on the field in order to get a good seat.

The stage was built on three flatbed trucks, and two refrigerator vans were used as dressing rooms. Somebody could have locked the doors and put the whole show on ice. I've often wondered if giving me a refrigerator van to dress in was some sort of commentary on the freshness of my material. All I kept thinking was if I'm not careful here, they could Birds Eye me and keep me for a whole new generation.

When our show started a nervous thing happened. They

*The end of the road—back to indoor plumbing. (NBC Photo by Gary Null)*

gave us a standing ovation. Picture, if you will, twenty thousand people in an audience suddenly standing up. It's frightening. I thought the island was tipping. There are only sixty thousand people in all of Guam. One out of three of them was in front of us. Think what I coulda done if the rating rigging man had been there. I opened with:

"Nice to be back on Guam. I drop in here every time we get lost on the way home.

"Guam is a very historic spot. This is where the Mutiny on the Bounty started. Captain Bligh wanted to *stay* here.

"You men really have an important job. We wouldn't want the Communists to capture all this crabgrass.

"I hear you guys are running out of targets. The last bombing raid destroyed two bridges and a truck convoy. I've been at officers' parties that did better than that."

We did a two-hour show. Everybody gave what must have been the last that was in him, and we were rewarded at the finish by another standing ovation. Guam is kinda hard to forget—it was like this audience had read the papers and knew where and what we had been doing for the last two weeks and were saying, "Thank you." Audiences like that get to you—especially after some of the groups I played to when I was starting in the business. Like some vaudeville houses in Chicago where if they liked you they didn't applaud, they just let you live.

Two years ago on Guam, after Janis Paige finished her number and received a tremendous ovation, a kid in the audience stood up and yelled, "Okay, let's really hear it for Janis." And everybody in the audience rose up and cheered and applauded, as Janis stood on stage not believing it, with tears streaming down her face.

Later she called home to her husband, Ray Gilbert, and said, "I'm coming home. Something happened to me today that I've waited for all my life. I heard this voice yell, and I saw this mass of humanity stand up, and I couldn't get my breath. Something caught me inside. I've worked twenty years in this business, and here I stand on an island called Guam in the middle of the Pacific . . . and this happens to me. If it never happens again and I never work again as long as I live, I don't care . . . I've never had anything like this in my life, and I'll never forget it, and nobody'll ever take it away from me! It's mine . . . all mine!"

Amen!

# CHAPTER THIRTEEN

Twenty-three thousand miles, twenty-four shows, and twelve days later, we arrived at the place we hold most cherished—L. A. Customs.

The battlefields behind us, we had finally reached the spot where the real fighting begins. Our adversaries were experienced, well-trained, capable, and tough, with all the efficiency of a housewife rifling her husband's pants the night after a poker game.

I have a theory about Customs men. I think they're frustrated baseball umpires who couldn't pass the physical. Take the one I drew. He towered under me by a good two feet and read my declaration form with all the trusting innocence of an income tax investigator. That man gave me a complete physical with just a stare. I was ready to confess to the diamonds I had hidden in my false heels, but I was wearing moccasins at the time. A look around me at my courageous cast showed me that they were undergoing the same scrutiny. A bead of perspiration dangled like a morning dewdrop from Jerry Colonna's mustache as one of the Customs men carefully and neatly piled his belongings in a sodden mass. A swipe of chalk on his suitcase, a sigh of relief from Colonna, and Jerry was safe. They hadn't found his postcards. History and the Professor had recorded that France had left its mark in Vietnam.

Clearing Customs might have been speedier if our group had been a bit more circumspect in their shopping. As the inspection continued, hordes of priceless impedimenta hove into view—rare hand-painted dishrags, burnished ashtrays magnificently fashioned by ancient twenty-year-old crafts-men from discarded shell casings, intricately woven pot holders, water pipes, pure rayon pajamas, Oriental type-writers fashioned into lamps, lamps fashioned into Oriental typewriters. . . . And the gems! Opals, rubies, sapphires by the hundreds, all bought at bargain basement prices at ten times the rate Woolworth's was asking. I gazed com-passionately at my troupe, they'd know better next time. An experienced traveler like myself doesn't fall into the trap of careless shopping. I had selected my trophies with care and with the eye of a man who's been around. I thought I detected a gleam of admiration in the eye of the Customs agent as he checked my treasures. After all, how many men in a mere twelve days can pick up a jade Buddha with a waterproof Timex in his belly, four ceramic neckties, and two shower mats from the royal bathroom in the palace in Bangkok?

On the way home from the airport, my modest tales of bravery convulsed my family, and it wasn't until Dolores inquired about my injured ankle that I realized why they weren't taking me seriously. I was so excited at seeing them again, I had forgotten to limp.

Actually, I had come out of the trip in pretty good shape. Aside from a head cold and a touch of dysentery, I was ready for the next war—and when I got to Revue the next morning, it was waiting for me. . . . A hundred and fifty thousand feet of film—twenty-four hours of eyeball fatigue to be axed down to an hour and a half, not counting commercials. Just *viewing* the footage took three days, eight hours a day. Our little epic made Tolstoy's *War and Peace* look like a trailer.

Having made so many contributions to the "Late Late Show" throughout the years, looking at film footage was no novelty to me, but the excitement of seeing the places we

*The Hopes pose for a family portrait, at an airport naturally.* (*NBC Photo by Gary Null*)

had been, and the faces of the boys we had entertained, made the first day of viewing fly by. I had instructed our crew to get as many shots of our audiences as they could, because I had felt that they were the real stars of our show—and the letters from parents who had seen their sons on my show bore me out.

As the viewing progresses an interesting game takes place as each of us tries to recall the names of some of the hundreds of officers we now have film on because once the stuff starts getting cut up into small pieces it is almost impossible to trace the locale of a particular shot. Also as

*It feels so good! (NBC Photo)*

the pace of editing increases they kind of put me on strings
and dance me from one movieola to another. One editor will
be showing me how he has cut together a section of Jerry
Colonna, and the minute he's finished they whisk me into
another cubicle to okay Joey Heatherton's number. Then
I'm wheeled into the projection room to look at some carrier
takeoffs for the opening of that sequence. After a few days
of this I have a good understanding of what puffed wheat
goes through.

Every shot we watched was being catalogued by our
librarian, Barry Parnell. Barry was not only a librarian,

he *looked* like one—thinning blond hair, pale blue eyes, and wearing a pair of Viennese-psychiatrist-type rimless glasses —this intellectually-appearing young man saved us countless man-hours with his precise filing. Whenever an obscure piece of footage was needed, Barry always managed to come up with it. If Barry had been around thirty-five years ago, Judge Crater would still be with us.

We were very lucky in assembling a fine crew of editors, because our show rolled in right at the height of the pilot season—the better film cutters were extremely independent, and neither money nor bribery could lure these Knights of the Scissors from their appointed surgery. There was only one road left open—I appealed to their patriotism . . . I told them about the faces of the boys their moms were waiting to see—about the men in the rice paddies in Vietnam—the trials, the hardships, the victories, the defeats. . . . When I got through Gomer Pyle never had a chance.

We had just two weeks to cut 150,000 feet down to nine thousand, and it took a crew of eighteen to do the job.

The editing rooms at Revue, or for that matter, anywhere, are the most uncomfortable hunks of architecture ever perpetrated by man—they are generally barren and cold and each piece of equipment has sharp corners specifically designed to gouge an unwary elbow or shin. The floor we had leased at Revue contained a maze of these chrome and steel rabbit warrens, and for two weeks I spent the best years of my life ducking into one or another.

If it weren't for the unfailing good nature of our Supervising Editor, Dick Belding, I don't think we'd have made it. When Dick and I didn't see eye to eye on the way a sequence should be cut, I would defer to his superior experience, and somehow or other it always came out the way I wanted it. Dick never could stand to see a grown man cry.

While I'm at it, I'd like to salute the rest of the celluloid

*"I suppose you wonder why I've called this meeting."* (NBC Photo by Frank Carroll)

snippers who shared our fate in Operation Frenzy . . . Lou Lombardo, Art Schneider, Gino Grimaldi, Art Ottinger, Monte Hellman, Noel Nosseck, and our very English co-ordinator, Alan Marks; the king of overtime, our negative cutter, Larry Watkins; and two guys who worked a non-stop thirty-six hours, our sound cutters, Jim Troutman and Art Klin.

I also owe a tip of the glass to Marvin Coyle, a veteran of many previous Battles of the Scissors; Bill Sterling, the congenial liaison man from Pacific Title; and to three executives at Revue who broke their backs to see that we had facilities, equipment, and studios at the height of their season, David J. O'Connell, Harry Garfield, and Joe Hyatt.

Inevitably, in an operation as large as ours, some film will turn up missing. Several years ago, when we did a show aboard one of our carriers in the Mediterranean, the U.S.S. *Forrestal* in Naples, we shot a sequence of Colonna and a cigarette-smoking monkey. It was a hilarious bit with the Professor hard put to keep his own against the ad-libbing chimp. That can of film never turned up, and it's better than even money that somewhere in Naples there's a monkey trying to sell the film for enough loot to buy his own organ grinder.

Now Box 20 was missing . . . you'd think that with 150,-000 feet of film, the disappearance of a thousand feet or so might be trivial—and well it might, except we don't know to this day what was in Box 20—it could have been the best piece in the show, and its disappearance still haunts me. . . . How do you think I feel knowing that fifteen minutes of my immortal sand dance, done with a bad ankle, might be lost to posterity forever?

Eight days later we had a rough cut of the show ready . . . really rough. According to Joan Maas, our very effi-cient production assistant, we were still eleven minutes too long. We didn't doubt Joan's accuracy, she's from Bolivar and she oughta know. For your incidental information

246

*"Who said that?"* (*NBC Photo by Frank Carroll*)

*aficionados*, Bolivar's a small town in Missouri. When I say small town I'm giving Bolivar the best of it—the only road there ends up a tree.

Cutting those eleven minutes was the most difficult part of the whole operation. We had seven stars on the show, and by trimming their appearances, we'd wreck everything. . . . . We had large amounts of footage covering the boys in the audiences at various bases, and we weren't about to cut that either. There was only one place left to cut, and choking back a sob, I did it. So if you know any exhibitor who's interested in eleven minutes of Colonna, Jack Jones, and myself in Edwardian costumes and long blond wigs singing "England Swings," drop me a line—you're in for 10 per cent.

The tedious part of the job was over, the show was cut to size, and now I just wanted to go somewhere to heal. The dubbing still remained to be done, but this was a chore I had planned to palm off on The Owl. The Owl is my associate producer, Mort Lachman, who achieved this fond monicker through his affinity for thick black-rimmed glasses. The glasses actually serve a cosmetic function, since the heavy frames conceal the black pouches beneath his orbs, which are his service stripes earned under fire in previous forays in the cutting room. Mort, incidentally, who has been with me for eighteen years, bears an astonishing resemblance to Steve Allen—with his glasses on, that is; without them he looks like a drunken raccoon.

My golf clubs were already in the trunk of my car when Mort informed me that I was needed for the dubbing session. I had forgotten that the show was to be knitted together by my narration. My running commentary served to identify the places we were at, and at the same time act as a bridge between the various pieces of entertainment. It meant viewing the show again and again, no tough chore for me, but, inevitably, little things would become apparent to me which would entail additional cutting. They finally solved this by having me wild-track the narration, and then let the technicians fit the sound track to the film footage.

Nobody has a higher regard for the technicians than I do —those Eye and Ear Specialists have saved me many times—and soundwise, this show was a real challenge. Filming outdoors as we did is technically a hazardous operation. . . . Even ace mixers like Dave Forrest can't cope with every emergency. . . . There was no way of knowing when a chopper would buzz us during a scene and drown out some of the dialogue . . . Or when a wind would whip up and muffle a song number. . . . It's here where the years of experience of people like Jim Stewart, our Chief Sound Engineer, really pay off. . . . Jim, with his vast technical knowledge, can make a diving F-104 sound like the purring of a pussycat. Without guys like this, our Vietnam Special would have sounded like tune-up day at Les Mans.

My favorite part of the show is what we call "The Tribute"—this sequence generally finishes the program and contains the most exciting footage. . . . It shows the men in various unguarded moments, in times of stress, when they're relaxed and laughing, when they're praying, when they're working and when they're fighting. It rarely runs for more than six minutes, but in it is contained the life of the combat man as we see him—it's the sort of thing that brings forth mixed emotions—like the shot of a GI perched in a tree viewing the show and sipping a beer—or a soldier with both legs in traction, laughing happily as Carroll Baker kisses him—or a flight of jets screaming off a carrier into the action. . . . It's difficult to write a suitable narration for this sort of thing, and I don't try to. . . . The best I can do is look at it and express what I feel as it runs. I might as well admit it, I have no politics where the boys are concerned. I only know that they're over there doing a job that has to be done, and whatever is best for them is best for me. I bow to no man in my love for my country, and if my zeal for backing these kids to the hilt means offending a few part-time citizens and thereby losing a few points in the Nielsen, so be it.

On January 16, three days before air time, we previewed our show for the press. I was extremely grateful to General Sarnoff for allowing us to use the closed-circuit facilities. But he had little choice. It was either that or be drafted. The show itself received gratifying reviews from the press, and some of them were ecstatic. And to this day I wonder if my closing remarks to them had anything to do with it. I said, "I have a great deal of faith in this show, and in you, ladies

*"Let go, I didn't mean it."* (*NBC Photo*)

and gentlemen of the press. And I hope you enjoy what you see. For those of you who give us a good review, I salute you now. And as for the bad reviews . . . I want to thank you Communists for coming, anyway."

That show received the highest rating a show of mine had ever achieved, and right while I was modestly demanding more money from my sponsor, some guy announced that he had rigged the rating. I had a tough decision to make. I didn't know whether to sue him or decorate him. According to his claim, he obtained the list of people right from the heart of the Nielsen's filing system—the garbage can. I was reasonably certain that my sponsor, Chrysler, didn't believe my high rating was influenced, but I admit I was worried. The day after it was announced, I sent my Imperial in for a checkup and a Plymouth came back.

It was about this time that I was invited to entertain at a dinner at the White House in honor of Henry Cabot Lodge. White House security being what it is, I was required to obtain a pass and enter through a specified gate. My mind was on my monologue because I promptly lost the pass and forgot the number of the gate. Undaunted, I appeared at the wrong gate and depended upon my profile to gain entry. The Guard recognized me all right, but insisted on my telling him a joke before he would pass me through. Caught with my idiot cards down, I was forced to ad lib that Lyndon was trying to convert Luci's fiancé, but the kid refused to become a Texan. . . . But he let me in anyway.

It was all-Vietnam night at the White House. Anita Bryant sang a special arrangement of "Battle Hymn of the Republic," which drew a standing ovation led by the President. When he stands, everybody stands. Also on the program were two marvelous young folk singers named Stephen Addiss and William Crofut. These kids leave behind their tremendously successful careers in theater, television, and college concerts to travel for the State Department in Kenya, Thailand, and Vietnam. And they don't entertain in the big cities; they go out into the small villages and sing to and with the people. In the words of our President: "They sought no soft and easy life . . . and by what they did, above and beyond what could be asked of them, Steve Addiss and Bill Crofut serve America and freedom in the very finest and proudest way."

The dinner was marked by two memorable goofs, both made by me. In introducing the celebrities, which included Robert McNamara, Dean Rusk and General Maxwell Taylor, I had forgotten to mention Martha Raye, and it wasn't until I sat down that I realized my omission. Anxious to

251

*Who's tired?* (*NBC Photo*)

right things, I jumped up to the microphone and started to introduce her. Unfortunately, the mike had been turned off. I was frantic. I knocked on the mike and yelled, "Give me some power! Give me some power!" Right then, Henry Cabot Lodge leaned over and said to me, "You've got a lot of nerve asking for power in this room!" which got a very big laugh, in fact, maybe the biggest laugh of the night. And then he said, "Bob, it's wonderful to see you and the next time you come over to stay in Vietnam please come and stay with me." Can you picture my cast and crew digging those arrangements, with me cooling it in luxury with the Ambassador and them sleeping on top of a pile of grenades at one of those high-rise (in the middle of the night) hotels?

I don't want to give you the idea that our Ambassador is living a quiet and restful life over there, because any night in Saigon can turn out to be the Fourth of July, and everybody runs for the cellar. But Henry Cabot Lodge survived Khrushchev, Oregon, and David Merrick, and is still ready and able to lay his life on the line for Uncle.

I thanked the Ambassador and assured him I'd let him know when I arrived. So he could hide the towels.

I'll probably go again, if I can pass the physical. I don't know that putting a little more mileage on this well-traveled hull will help win the war, but if it makes one person feel better, it's worth it. Even if that one person is only me.

I guess I've faced more of our guys than a medium-size enemy ever does. I've seen them under all sorts of conditions. I've met them in their place of business . . . they deal in hardship and pain. And fear and sometimes death are their companions. And the thing that never stops amazing me is the good grace with which they accept their impossible roles. A soldier stands in the twilight between his civilization and the raw savagery of war.

When you can give these kids a laugh or hear them cheer an American gal, you feel lucky that Max Factor smiled on ya'.

Here's a letter a kid on the *Ticonderoga* handed us as we left:

*"Dear Bob:*
"You, no doubt, would like to know how a serviceman feels about his duty in Vietnam! I would like to say, I feel what we are doing is needed, and one of the necessary evils of being one of the major powers of today's world.

"As to the question of backing, I have just shaken hands with and been encouraged by Carroll Baker, Anita Bryant and Diana

*He missed the show. (NBC Photo by Gary Null)*

Lynn Batts (Miss U.S.A.). With backing like this, do you think a few imbeciles burning their draft cards can really affect us?

"We had a great time meeting all of you.

"Merry Christmas. Thanks."

[Signed] Neal H. Lampman
O.I. Div.
USS Ticonderoga CVA 14
C/o FPO, San Francisco, Calif.

These kids seem to be a lot more optimistic about this commitment than a lot of our citizens here at home. In their everyday job of fighting this treacherous war they know there's no alternative. . . . They know that in this shrinking world the perimeter of war is boundless.

Usually you hear a serviceman say, "I got fifty-two more days before I go home." But a lot of these guys are too busy fighting for their lives to stop and count days till they can go back to Shangri-la. They're not about to give up—because they know if they walked out of this bamboo obstacle course it would be like saying to the Commies—"Come and get it."

There's all kinds of American guys over there, all doing different jobs. All making some kind of sacrifice. And it made you proud to meet and share the holidays with them. Everybody agreed it was a ball, and for me personally I have to lift a little bit of Will Rogers and say, "I've never met a GI I didn't like."